A FINE KETTLE OF FISH

AND 150 OTHER
ANIMAL EXPRESSIONS

by MICHAEL MACRONE

MJF BOOKS
NEW YORK

Published by MJF Books
Fine Communications
Two Lincoln Square
60 West 66th Street
New York, NY 10023

A Fine Kettle of Fish
Copyright © 1995 by Cader Company, Inc., and Michael Macrone

Isbn 1-56731-458-9
LC Control No.01-130251

This book was previously published as *Animalogies*.

Manufactured in the United States of America on acid-free paper

MJF Books and the MJF colophon are trademarks of
Fine Creative Media, Inc.

10   9   8   7   6   5   4   3   2   1

Table of Contents

Change Its Spots • Mrs. O'Leary's Cow • A Scapegoat • To Separate Sheep from Goats • A Snake in the Grass • To Strain at a Gnat • A Swan Song

Raining Cats and Dogs

Any Man Who Hates Dogs and Babies Can't Be All Bad • To Bark up the Wrong Tree • Beware of the Dog • Bowwow • A Cynic • Dog Days • Dog Eat Dog • Every Dog Has Its Day • To Go to the Dogs • Hair of the Dog • A Hangdog Look • His Bark Is Worse Than His Bite • Hot Dog • Let Sleeping Dogs Lie • Love Me, Love My Dog • Man Bites Dog • To Put on Dog • A Shaggy-Dog Story • An Underdog • To Rain Cats and Dogs • To Bell the Cat • A Cat's Nine Lives • A Cat's-Paw • Kitty-Corner • To Let the Cat out of the Bag • Like a Cat on a Hot Tin Roof • Not Room Enough to Swing a Cat • Sitting in the Catbird Seat • There's More Than One Way to Skin a Cat • When the Cat's Away, the Mice Will Play

Silly Geese : Odd Animal Phrases

Adam's Off Ox • To Beard the Lion in Its Den • Beating a Dead Horse • A Charley Horse • To Cook One's Goose • A Dingbat • An Elephant Never Forgets • To Go Whole Hog • Groundhog Day • Hogwash • Hush Puppies • A Kangaroo Court • A Lounge Lizard • Moth-Eaten • Pig Latin • To Ride a High Horse • Round Robin • Snake Oil • Take the Bull by the Horns • A Teddy Bear • Till the Cows Come Home • Two Shakes of a Lamb's Tail

Introduction

Bats are blind, clams happy, and groundhogs prescient. Even cautious fraidy-cats have nine lives to spare. Bears lick their cubs into shape but kill their prey with hugs. Chickens are chicken (except when they're cocky), and dodos were dodos before they died off.

Thus we're assured by centuries, or at least decades, of animal lore; but is any of it true? The history of such sayings and their merits are the subjects of *Animalogies,* whose title is shorthand for both "animal analogies" and "animal etymologies." In the following pages I'll examine the meanings and origins of some of the best-known and most clichéd assertions about our furry and feathered friends and enemies—from shaggy dogs to catbirds, Charley horses to scapegoats, Spanish flies to paper tigers.

Along the way you'll learn about the mysterious lemmings of Norway, alleged to commit suicide in droves. You'll find out whether ostriches really stick their heads in the sand, whether elephants ever forget, and whether opossums truly "play possum." You'll discover the origin of such fabulous beasts as the bugbear, the dingbat, and Welsh rabbit. You'll be surprised by little-known facts, for example that they used to hang dogs as criminals and that red herrings were once used to foil rival huntsmen.

•

This book covers but a small sample of the thousands of animalogies from the annals of English, let alone other tongues. The plenitude of comparisons—to pigs and cats, dogs and bats, sharks and sheep, bulls and bears—isn't just a remnant of mankind's history of farming and hunting. It's also an index of how we measure ourselves against other members of the animal kingdom.

We see ourselves as like enough to animals that we may project our feelings on them: thus wasps are *angry* and cats *curious.* And we regularly use them as mirrors of human behavior: cruel hypocrites are like the weeping crocodile, mischievous children are "little monkeys." Similar analogies to plants and rocks are pretty rare.

Yet at the same time we treat animals as completely separate—and lower—in the chain of being. (Otherwise, we wouldn't eat them.) To "act like an animal" is to succumb to a baser nature, to erase the crucial distinction of man from beast. Far more animalogies are insults than are compliments, as a quick skim of this book (especially the last chapter) will prove.

It's the interplay of similarity and difference that makes animal behavior so intriguing, and which has inspired moral allegories from Aesop's to Orwell's. They ask the question, Could people *really* act like that? and answer, Unfortunately, yes. The oldest phrases in this book, in fact, derive from Aesop, and many others are meant to teach lessons. Most such animalogies (*The early*

*bird catches the worm; You can't teach an old dog new
tricks*) are obvious and dull and therefore aren't included.

•

In addition to the ethical variety, there are many just
plain silly animal expressions, which please us because
they're incongruous—because it's *funny* to think of people as animals. *Ham actor* and *lounge lizard* are in this
category, as are most of the entries in the fifth chapter,
"Silly Geese." (Whether the phrase or the animal is more
important determines how chapters are alphabetized.)

Not every phrase in this book is an animal/human
analogy; several (such as *hair of the dog* and *snake oil*)
refer to animal parts or products that have become
metaphors. Nor do they end there; it sometimes seems as
though there's an animal to fill every metaphorical need:
temporal (*till the cows come home, in two shakes of a
lamb's tail, Groundhog Day*); spatial (*kitty-corner, beeline,
as the crow flies*); epistemological (*a pig in a poke, neither
fish nor fowl, pigeonhole*); political (*dark horse, lame
duck, kangaroo court*); culinary (*hush puppies, hot dog,
Welsh rabbit*); etc.

•

I acknowledge my most useful references in the
"Sources" appendix. I'd also like to thank Michael
Cader, Philip Reynolds, Catherine Karnow, Thorina
Rose, and Lori Lipsky for their advice and support. This
book is dedicated to Clea and Didot.

Acting like an Animal

This chapter covers the most basic type of animal analogy: the direct comparison of man to beast. In school such phrases—"loose *as* a goose," "crazy *like* a fox"—are called similes, from the Latin for "same."

But how similar, really, are the two sides of the equation? That depends on what the phrase is intended to mean—there are lots of ways to be "loose." It also depends on whether our assumptions about animal behavior are true. As we shall see, they're often not.

The phrases in this section are alphabetized by animal.

BLIND AS A BAT

Bats may not have the best eyes in the world, but they're hardly "blind." This error springs from the fact that bright light bothers them—for the original saying was *blind as a bat at noon*.

In fact, bats are quite capable of using their eyes if the sun isn't in them; it's an evolutionary bonus that they can also navigate by natural sonar, emitting squeals and listening for echoes. Because they "see" as well in the dark as in the light, most (but not all) bats prefer to keep late hours, when things are quieter, which is rather sensible.

Bats' nocturnal life-style, eerie cries, and general ugliness give people the creeps, without a lot of good reason. By and large they pose no threat to human beings; their diet is made up mostly of fruit and insects, with the occasional small animal for variety. On the other hand, there are a few nastier breeds native to Central and South America. These are the blood-sucking "vampire" bats, found nowhere else in the world—not even in Eastern Europe, home of the vampire legends.

Vampire bats seem to prefer the blood of chickens, cows, and horses to human blood, but attacks on people aren't unheard of. And in fact, if a vampire bat takes a liking to your hemoglobins you can expect it to come calling for more. Luckily, if you're asleep you'll never feel a thing, as its saliva acts as a local anaesthetic.

LIKE A BAT OUT OF HELL

The logic of this one's trickier than you'd think. Because bats prefer the dark, when ghosts, goblins, and other spooky creatures are about, they've always been regarded as friends of the devil. So that explains why they're in hell in the first place.

The problem is that we almost always use this phrase to describe somebody's running as fast as possible *away* from someplace. Why would a bat, presumably right at home, flee the inferno? Some authorities have suggested that the phrase alludes to bats' hatred of light, in which instance they'd *really* hate the glare of hellfire. But since there's always hellfire in hell, it's hard to explain why they'd go there at all. It would make more sense if the phrase referred to a hell-bent bat zooming about on some mission for the devil himself.

Whatever, most experts think that the saying originated as slang for "really fast" in the British Royal Flying Corps during World War I. But it's likely that the phrase had already been floating in the air, since some apparently heard it Stateside around the turn of the century.

A BEAR HUG

We may use this phrase for big cuddles, but all it used to mean was the deadly embrace of a real live bear. The fact, as people eventually figured out, is that while bears have been known to smack around those who disturb their peace, they don't "hug" anything except maybe trees.

Where the notion came from is impossible to say; probably just from fevered imaginations. Among the strongest animals alive, bears mostly work with their bare paws, striking prey dead with a single swipe. Then they feast—though rare is the case of their eating people, whose flesh is not to their taste.

Nevertheless, I wouldn't go out of my way to insult a bear, especially not a grizzly, whose weight typically approaches half a ton. On the other hand, grizzly bears are poor tree climbers, so make that your first escape route. The only bear that could follow you up is a black bear, but they're generally peaceable.

TO LICK INTO SHAPE

The very wise yet very error-prone Pliny the Elder, the famous ancient naturalist, wrote in his great work that "Bears when first born are shapeless masses of white flesh a little larger than mice, their claws alone being prominent. The mother then licks them gradually into proper shape" (*Natural History*, book 8). Pliny wasn't the first to observe this "fact"; it goes at least as far back as Aristotle, whose theories dominated philosophy and science for about 2,000 years.

The notion is of course ridiculous. Newborn bears are no more "shapeless" than most mammals at that stage; and lots of animals lick their young; but nobody makes the same claim for housecats. One can only suppose that, given mama bears' protectiveness, none of the old experts got close enough to a newborn cub to really know.

Whether everybody really bought this idea is unknown, but it was good enough for a metaphor. In Shakespeare's *Henry the Sixth, Part 3*, for example, the Duke of Gloucester (later Richard III) complains of his deformities, likening himself "to a chaos, or an unlick'd bear-whelp / That carries no impression like the dam [mother]" (act 3, scene 2). Less loftily, we still talk of things that need to be "licked into shape," but have forgotten the part about the bears.

TO MAKE A BEELINE

Have you ever seen a bee fly in a straight line? Apparently Edgar Allan Poe did, for he defined *beeline* that way in "The Gold Bug" (1843). But Henry David Thoreau saw it differently; only nine years later he wrote

in *Autumn* of "a bee-line, a waving and sinuous line right and left."

As anyone familiar with both men's work knows, Poe's was the more imaginative and metaphorical of the two, but Thoreau's the more thoughtful and considered. A bee's flight is more often than not leisurely and variable, with frequent stops and detours. In other words, it isn't much of a "line" at all. However, it is true that sometimes the bee can be a regular little bullet, as when it's loaded up on some especially sweet pollen and hastens home to the hive. The exception rather than the rule has dominated the history of this expression.

TO GIVE THE BIRD

Though Americans of a certain age think this means "make an obscene gesture," *giving the bird* has historically signified something else, albeit something equally unpleasant.

The present saying is a more general form of what

began, in 19th-century theatrical parlance, as *to give the goose* or simply *to goose*. The original reference was to the unpleasant hissing noise geese make when angry, a nice parallel to the hisses aimed at lame actors by unsatisfied audiences.

For a while in the later 1800s, giving the goose was actually verboten in American theaters. But this silly prohibition didn't last long, and the goose is alive and well on both sides of the Atlantic. (Don't confuse it with *egging on*, which has no connection to goose eggs, deriving rather from the old verb *to edge*.)

Back to more interesting matters: the obscene meaning of *giving* or *flipping the bird* originated in the late '60s and was first recorded as slang by enterprising lexicographers at the University of South Dakota. They traced it to student argot at New Mexico State but offered no explanation of what birds have to do with middle fingers.

LIKE A BULL IN A CHINA SHOP

This phrase sure *sounds* like it should spring from some quaint and twisted tale, and language experts have industriously supplied them. Among the more plausible theories is that *bull in a china shop* (coined circa 1830) refers way back to Aesop's fable of the ass in the pottery shop. The only problem with this idea is that an ass isn't a bull nor pottery china.

Farther out is Charles Funk's version, in which Aesop's fable offered a theme to some (unknown) British political cartoonist. According to Funk, who's basically making this up, said cartoonist cleverly transformed the ass into John Bull (the British equivalent of Uncle Sam), who was poised to rampage through the Chinese empire if trade relations broke down. Funk continues:

> The episode may have been the failure of Lord Amherst's diplomatic mission to China in 1816, or the events may have to do with the termination of the monopoly by the East India Company, in 1834, of trade with China. The cartoonist may have been some such political satirist as George Cruikshank, or the earlier caricaturists, James Gillray or Thomas Rowlandson.

Needless to say, this book will be entirely free of such wild speculations.

Sadly, *bull in a china shop* really does just mean what it says. But the experts do have to earn their keep.

TO SEE RED

Red, they say, drives otherwise peaceable bulls to a raging frenzy, especially if a matador is waving that color cape in their faces. Actually, cattle—like all mammals save human beings and monkeys—are practically color-blind; they couldn't care less whether your hankie is red or raspberry. What gets them riled in the bullring isn't the cape's color but all the prancing and waving. I can't tell you how old this error is, but the metaphor *see red* traces to the turn of the 20th century.

TO FIGHT LIKE KILKENNY CATS

Maybe they do make cats meaner in Ireland. But tales about the ferocious felines of Kilkenny (a southeastern county) are probably just leg-pulling, or tail-pulling.

Here are a few samples. The best-known legend concerns two Kilkenny cats so mutually disenchanted that they fought in a sawpit until all that was left were their tails. There's a good old limerick on the subject:

> There once were two cats of Kilkenny,
> Which thought there was one cat too many,
>   So they mewed and they bit,
>   And they scratched and they fit,
> Till, excepting their nails and the tips of their tails,
> Instead of two cats there weren't any.

A variation on this theme involves Hessian soldiers garrisoned in Kilkenny at the turn of the 19th century, during the Irish rebellion. Some fun-loving privates sported with a pair of kitties by tying their tails together, hanging them over a rope, and watching them go at it. Officers in the garrison heard rumors about the "fun" and sent a spy to investigate.

When the troops heard the not-very-discreet snooper climbing the stairs, one of them cleverly cut the cats apart by their tails. The cats jumped howling out the window just as the spy barged in. When he demanded an explanation for the remaining tails, the private who'd severed them invented the now-familiar story: two Kilkenny cats were fighting so fiercely they couldn't be stopped, and they eventually ate each other up.

Another legend tells of a great battle in the later 18th century that drew in all the cats of County Kilkenny, plus allies from around Ireland. When all was meowed and done, a thousand cats lay dead on the battlefield.

Who knows where such stories came from, but there have been a few attempts to turn them into allegories. Some point to the intense rivalry between the towns of Kilkenny and Irishtown, which resulted in a bitter and destructive series of skirmishes between the 14th and 17th centuries.

TO GRIN LIKE A CHESHIRE CAT

One of the best-loved literary creatures has to be Lewis Carroll's Cheshire cat, from his satiric *Alice's Adventures in Wonderland* (1865). It can appear and disappear at will, in whole or in parts—as in this, his most famous disappearing act:

> [The cat] vanished quite slowly, beginning with
> the end of the tail, and ending with the grin, which
> remained some time after the rest of it had gone.
>
> "Well! I've often seen a cat without a grin,"
> thought Alice; "but a grin without a cat! It's the
> most curious thing I ever saw in all my life!"
> (Chapter 6)

We owe the popular image of the cat and its fixed yet
inscrutable smile to this scene; yet Carroll invented neither the creature nor its grin. (He did make it talk and
disappear, though.) Ten years before *Alice*, William
Makepeace Thackeray had already written, "That woman
grins like a Cheshire cat" (*The Newcomes*). We find even
earlier references in writings of the late 18th century.

In fact, the simile is an old one, so old (and so common)
its origins are lost. Our sources do suggest a few possibili-
ties, though. Some say that once upon a time Cheshire
cheese wasn't sold in a wheel but in the shape of a cat's
smiling puss. (The cat was happy because Cheshire was
exempt from royal taxation.) Others claim the cheese was
sold imprinted with a poorly rendered coat of arms, its lion
looking more like a grimacing tabby than a menacing leo.
(In one variation on this tale, the "artist" was a Cheshire
sign painter.) Still others say the phrase actually refers to
the terrifying smirk of a certain Cheshire forest ranger
named *Cat*erling who lived in the reign of Richard III.

Alas, all of these are probably bunk. No matter; however the notion appeared, it was Carroll who made it famous, and who also made the Cheshire cat disappear, leaving only its famous grin.

HAPPY AS A CLAM

What makes this jolly little mollusk so happy? And how could you tell, anyway? Perhaps by its vaguely smiley "mouth," which inspired New Englanders of the 19th century to shout "Shut your clamshell!" at talkative fellows. (This is the ancestor of *Clam up!*)

But of course clams don't really smile or make any other sort of expression with their shells. The true origin of *happy as a clam,* which was in circulation by the 1830s, is the more descriptive saying *happy as a clam at high water* or *high tide,* when clamming is most difficult. If you were a clam washed up on a beach, you wouldn't be very merry.

Besides lending us this colorful simile, clams have served as models of less flattering human traits. You wouldn't want to be called "as tight as a clam," for instance, and Mark Twain intended no praise when he referred to someone in his *Sketches* (1872) as an "intellectual clam."

CROCODILE TEARS

Among the most dangerous of reptiles—far more threatening than its brother the alligator—is the wily crocodile, which is quite capable of making a snack out of the careless. (Especially bad are African crocs, found mostly in the Nile.) Called "a curse on four legs" by the Roman naturalist Pliny the Elder (first century A.D.), crocodiles were long believed to lure unwary prey by weeping and wailing, as if in distress.

This notion dates to about the fourth century but wasn't coined in English writings until the 16th. A typical citation is this, from the Reverend Edward Topsell's *History of Serpents* (1608): "There are not many brute beasts that can weep, but such is the nature of the Crocodile, that to get a man within his danger, he will sob, sigh & weep, as though he were in extremity, but suddenly he destroyeth him. Others say, that the crocodile weepeth after he hath devoured a man."

Topsell was neither the first nor the last to be confused on this point. Do crocodiles shed tears craftily, to lure

unwary prey, or do they slay first and weep later? Shakespeare, among others, seemed to believe the former, but recent usage prefers the latter. Either way, nobody believed the grief was real, and the important point is that crocodile tears are hypocritical, a mock show of sorrow from the instigator himself.

The saying has no basis in fact, however. Crocodiles can make an awful noise, but they don't shed actual tears.

LIKE WATER OFF A DUCK'S BACK

"When men are men of the world," wrote the Englishman Charles Kingsley in 1863, "hard words run off them like water off a duck's back." Like Kingsley, we use the phrase mostly to praise indifference (or machismo) in the face of fortune's slings and arrows.

It's true enough that ducks pay little mind to the water on their backs, which rolls right off. (In fact, they take to water like a duck to water.) But they're hardly the only (or the oldest) example of animal stoicism; similar phrases, with different animals, were common well before the present phrase made its appearance in the earlier 19th century.

The obscure Greek dramatist Cephisodorus, for example, coined the phrase *like rain off an ass* around 400 B.C., and it became a classical proverb. Only slightly more recent is the variant *as much as a tortoise bothers about flies*. Though in circulation as late as the Renaissance, neither phrase ultimately made the cut, and *like water off a duck's back* is now the standard.

TO PLAY DUCKS AND DRAKES

If it walks like a duck and quacks like a duck, it's probably a duck—unless it's a drake, the special name for the female of the species. But what ducks of either gender have to do with *playing ducks and drakes* (which now means "to squander" or "act recklessly") is unclear, beyond the fact that the game originally involved water.

According to our earliest English source (1583), there was once "a kind of sport or play with an oyster shell or stone thrown into the water, and making circles [as] it sinks; it is called a duck and a drake, and a half-penny cake." Maybe there was originally some analogy between a stone's skipping over water and a duck's swimming, but this is basically a nonsense rhyme—at least the cake part. It did catch on, though, as later that century the game became a metaphor for throwing away perfectly good money. If anyone's interested in playing, I'm available.

Also only tenuously related to the waterfowl is the verb *to duck*, which many people imagine refers to the way ducks duck under water to avoid danger. The true origin, though, is the old German verb *tauchen*, "to dive," via the Dutch modification *duiken*. If anything, the animal takes its name from the verb rather than vice versa.

CRAZY LIKE A FOX

If you've got to be crazy, you should be crazy like a fox, which is actually a compliment. In this case *crazy* means "shrewd" or "cunning" rather than "mad." The saying traces to the early 20th century, but *fox* has been an English epithet for crafty operators for about a thousand years. (Only recently has it come to denote a certain kind of attractive female.)

Less complimentary are such phrases as *crazy as a coot* or *crazy as a loon,* two very odd water birds. (I don't know which is worse, but loons cackle in the most disturbing way.) More puzzling is the phrase *crazy as a bedbug,* since these insects are neither obviously loony nor capable of foxiness. The scholar of slang Eric Partridge speculates that the phrase originates in the fact that bedbugs "make one 'itch like crazy.'"

LOOSE AS A GOOSE

Somewhere along the line, geese got a reputation for naughtiness. This is rather unfair, for while they're as sexually active as any fowl, they apparently are also faithful to their mates, with whom they live for life. Nonetheless, when *loose as a goose* was coined, it meant "hot to trot."

Today it means pretty much the opposite: "really

relaxed." It was in the 1960s that people began using *loose* as an antonym of "uptight"; this sense first appears (in the phrase *hang loose*) in a book by current hypernovelist Robert Coover. The meanings "wanton, dissolute, immoral, lecherous" are considerably older, dating to the 15th century.

SILLY GOOSE

Here are some of the things *silly* has meant since the 13th century: "saintly," "innocent," "harmless," "pathetic," "feeble," "rustic," "ignorant," "lowly," "stunned," and "foolish." So what *silly goose* means sort of depends; unfortunately, nobody knows exactly when or by whom it was coined.

But, as usual, there a plenty of theories. One is that the phrase is just one of many meaning "poor defenseless beast," as in *silly little lamb* or *poor silly mouse.* One count against this is that geese aren't really poor and defenseless. Better is the notion that geese have often been regarded as fairly imbecilic birds; in fact, *goose* was slang for "clown" as early as the 16th century. "Shall I stand still," asks a homily of the period, "like a goose or a fool, with a finger in my mouth?"

Our first written record paints a different picture. A proverb collection of the 19th century includes the saying "A goose is a silly bird—too much for one, not enough for two." This was allegedly the response of a Walsall resident when asked if he and his wife were planning on cooking a goose for Christmas. If so, we can add the definition "useless" to our list.

A HACK

Why are writers-for-hire called "hacks"? The answer is found in Hackney, the English town that lent its name to the original taxicabs. These were smallish carriages drawn by low-bred horses, themselves soon called hacks.

From town to carriage to horse to metaphor: in the 18th century *hack* became slang for low or disreputable types who (like the old cabbies) offered their services strictly for hire. Two particular targets of the figure were prostitutes and later the ink-stained wretches who churned out prose for a pitiful living.

The older meaning survives in New York, where those wacky cab drivers are still affectionately called hacks or "hackies."

A HAM ACTOR

Bad acting is ancient, but the first true hams were the blackfaced minstrels of the later 1800s. Subtle they were not, and among those who took a dim view of their antic overacting was the now-forgotten author of the popular tune "The Hamfat Man." The title refers to the minstrels' use of hog grease to clean the black off their faces.

It's very likely that the tune inspired the phrase *ham actor* or *ham* for short, although such epithets as *hamfat man* or *hamfat actor* may predate it. In any case "ham" appeared on its own by 1882, when someone referred to himself, in a letter to *Illustrated Sports and Drama News*, as "no ham, but a classical banjo player." Hello?

There are a couple of other hypotheses. It's possible that *ham* derives from *amateur*, either because Cockneys pronounce the word with an initial *h*, or just because the pun is appropriately bad. Less likely, but more amusing, is the notion that ham is short for "Hamlet," a role regularly butchered by hams.

A HOG ON ICE

On the rare occasion when this phrase is used today, it tends to mean "cocky" or "stubbornly independent." But as anyone who's observed the actual scene can tell you, hogs are not built for skating. Better, then, is the sense "awkward, inept," examples of which go back almost as far.

The expression in its former sense may be Scottish, referring to curling rather than swine. The sport, resembling shuffleboard or bocce, consists of sliding flat stones over an icy surface. Apparently, stones that stopped short were once called *hogs*, after their stubbornness.

Also possible is the theory cited in the *Morris Dictionary of Word and Phrase Origins*: In an effort to evade a roundup, sometimes a clever hog will get himself out on thin ice, where it is too dangerous to go fetch him. Of course, it can't get off by itself, either. "So anyone who steadfastly refused badly needed help or advice—perhaps to his own detriment—was said to be independent as a hog on ice."

LIKE LEMMINGS TO THE SEA

For an animal almost no one has seen, the lemming makes for an oddly popular metaphor. You can almost count on its popping up in comments on self-destructive group behavior, which is regularly likened to the mad rush of lemmings from the hills of Norway to their death by drowning in the sea.

Some have attempted to write off lemming suicide as a myth. Indeed, reports have been exaggerated, but

they're not false. Lemmings are perhaps best distinguished by their zeal to breed, a task at which they so excel that about every four years they overpopulate their habitat. Whole lemming populations develop a bad case of claustrophobia, not to mention desperate hunger.

Their dire situation prompts them to run from the hills—only they never stop running. Maniacally, the rodents jump every obstacle and swim every fjord, pressing on until there's nowhere farther to press, dying in massive numbers along the way, either by drowning, trampling, or disease. Only a few make it as far as the ocean, but those that do keep on going.

Actually, lemmings aren't bad swimmers, and a few survive the outing, landing somewhere solid before the craze wears off. But then again most of them die. Not that they *want* to die, which is really what's wrong with the popular notion. They probably have all sorts of other ideas, none of which (unfortunately) holds water.

TO STICK YOUR HEAD IN THE SAND

Everybody knows that ostriches are cowardly and not very bright. Throw a little scare into one, and it will find the nearest soft spot in the sand and stick its head right in—presumably on the theory that what you can't see won't hurt you.

But in this particular everybody's wrong. No ostrich

has ever been observed sticking its head into anything deeper than a feedbag. Where the idea came from, I can't say, except to note that it's true ostriches don't like fights. When threatened they first try to hide by stretching out on the ground, and when that fails they run. They're not bad runners, either, sometimes reaching a speed of 40 miles per hour. Unfortunately, this is about 30 m.p.h. slower than a hungry leopard.

Where ostriches really excel is in size; they're the biggest and heaviest of living birds, with African natives sometimes reaching heights of eight feet and weights of 300 pounds. They also deliver mighty kicks, lay the biggest eggs, and eat practically anything they're offered—including unwholesome things such as sharp metal objects. The only thing small about an ostrich is its brain.

A STOOL PIGEON

Homing pigeons are extremely dutiful once trained; the hard part is catching them in the first place. Since they like to flock together, one crude but effective method is to tie one pigeon to a stool as a lure. This is in fact what fowlers and hunters did in the 18th century, giving rise to the expression *stool pigeon* for "bait" or "decoy."

It didn't take long for bad guys to get their hands on the phrase, using it for a crook who'd been "turned" by the cops and was working to lure fellow criminals into the clutches of the law. Over the course of the 19th century *stool pigeon* was broadened to include any *jailbird* (17th century) who sang the authorities' tune. In other words, the "stoolie" didn't have to lead a flock to the cops, just lead the cops to their coop.

TO PLAY POSSUM

The opossum, a marsupial (pouched mammal), behaves rather oddly under threat. It falls flat on the ground in a faint, eyes closed, mouth open, and tongue hanging; it takes some investigating to tell it's still breathing.

People say the critters are putting on a show to fool their predators—that possums agree with Shakespeare's Falstaff: discretion is the better part of valor. Unfortunately, there are some possum predators that don't care one way or the other whether the critter is living or dead, and which would rather avoid the messy job of chase and kill if possible. More likely is that opossums are just stupendous cowards and that they're not "playing possum" at all but are actually frightened half to death.

TO RAT ON

Whenever rats got their reputation as tattle-tales, it was only about a century ago that *rat* became thieves' slang for an informer. The use of *to rat* meaning "to snitch" followed in due course.

This wasn't the first time the rodent was verbed, however. Since the early 19th century *rat* had meant "to turn coat, to desert one's party for the enemy." *The Oxford English Dictionary* traces this usage to the belief that rats are the first to jump off a sinking ship.

But even when that's so, I'm not sure what it's supposed to prove, since it isn't the rats who are steering. Furthermore, unlike the captain, there isn't much they could do to save the ship anyway. The whole notion that there's something treacherous about rats deserting a ship they weren't welcome on in the first place is a little ridiculous.

A BLACK SHEEP

Black sheep, much rarer than the white and tan kinds, were once the bane of the English wool industry, which is why they now stand for the embarrassment of any clan.

Before chemists perfected the art of dyeing and the lit-

tle black dress became a fashion essential, there was little a farmer could do with black sheep except eat them.
Their wool was worthless—it couldn't be dyed white, and
there just weren't enough black sheep to produce a useful quantity of black wool.

It didn't help that people believed that bad black
sheep scared the good white ones, or that their blackness
was the devil's work. So, all in all, the poor creatures took
a big hit in public opinion, through no fault of their own.

A SHREW

This unaffectionate term for a fierce, bossy woman actually comes from one of the shyest and tiniest of rodents.
Shrews, rarely seen in the open, are smaller even than mice;
in fact, pygmy shrews are the smallest living mammals.

But size isn't everything. Shrews have huge appe-
tites, which sometimes overcomes their shyness. A
shrew, which can starve in less than a day, will typically eat its weight in food every couple of hours. Generally
shrews feed on insects, but if they're hungry enough
they'll attack anything that moves, including other
shrews. In short, they're pugnacious little critters.

Metaphorical uses go back to the earliest days of the
English language, when the term applied equally to men
as to women. (Female-specific usage dates to about the
time of Chaucer.) Also deriving from this animalogy is

shrewd, which originally meant "shrewlike" or "vicious." Later it came to signify "sharp-tongued" and further along the line "sharp-witted," thus reversing from insult to compliment.

TO TALK TURKEY

This phrase goes back to pioneer days when turkeys were a staple of trade between palefaces and redskins. So *to talk turkey* meant "to talk *about* turkeys," not to gobble.

There's a good story about a Yankee hunter and his Indian friend on a birdhunt. Together they bagged four turkeys and four crows; but it was the Yankee who divided the booty. "A turkey for me, a crow for you" was his basic procedure. "You talk all turkey for you," protested his partner; "only talk crow for Indian! Now I talk turkey to you!" Needless to say, the final split was more even.

This alleged incident allegedly inspired the use of *talk turkey* to mean "deal plainly." Though later the animalogy took on additional senses, such as "speak pleasantly" or "speak pompously," by the turn of the century it pretty much meant only "get down to business." Except, that is, in the charming Southernism, *say pea-turkey*—as in, "She didn't say pea-turkey to me."

The World's Your Oyster

In the last chapter we considered direct comparisons; in this we examine metaphors, which are more indirect and symbolic. A good example is the first entry, *an albatross,* a literary symbol for an unshakable burden.

Some of these phrases, like similes, are based on conceptions and misconceptions about animal behavior in general. Others have to do with particular stories or incidents. *Spelling bee,* for example, refers to the characteristic social habits of bees, while *canard* and *ugly duckling* originate in literature and history. What all the phrases included here have in common is that an animal name has taken on new life as a figure of speech.

The phrases in this section are alphabetized by animal.

AN ALBATROSS

The albatross is pretty large as seabirds go, about four feet long with a wingspan of up to four yards. You certainly wouldn't want anything that big (and heavy) around your neck, but there are a lot of things you wouldn't want around your neck, so why *albatross*?

The reason lies in Samuel Taylor Coleridge's poem "The Rime of the Ancient Mariner" (1798), which has been forced on generations of students. Coleridge tells of the seafaring superstition that it is bad luck to kill an albatross, which embodies the spirit of a sailor lost at sea. The narrator makes this goof, and the consequences aren't pretty—he must constantly relive and retell his mistake. Thus *albatross* has come to mean "curse" or "unrelenting burden."

Visitors to San Francisco may be amused to know that *albatross* putatively stems from the Spanish *alcatraz*, "large pelican," perhaps by assimilation with the Latin *alba*, "white," its color. (Other theories available upon request.) That they are not graceful and have a hard time lifting off accounts for their nickname, *gooney birds*.

TO HAVE BATS IN YOUR BELFRY

Imagine the feeling of being trapped in a hall of mirrors; that's sort of how a bat feels in a belltower, or "belfry."

The reason, as we've seen (page 2), is that bats rely largely on sonar to get around. Small, encircling, echoey spaces like belfries are rather apt to give them the jitters, not because they're claustrophobic, but because they can't handle the information overload. Every way they turn they encounter echoes upon echoes, and if you watched them try to navigate you'd certainly think they'd lost their senses—zigging, zagging, darting, pulling up, spinning about, and generally getting nowhere fast.

Thus the early–20th-century coinage *bats in the belfry,* meaning "crazed." It first turns up around 1901 in G. W. Peck's *Peck's Red-Headed Boy*: "They all thought a crazy man with bats in his belfry had got loose." There's an

obvious analogy of the top of a tower to the top of a human; in fact, *belfry* soon came to be used on its own as a humorous metaphor for "head."

Likewise the first half of the phrase would come into its own as *bats* and *batty,* meaning "nuts." First used this way in 1903, *batty* was actually coined circa 1595 by Shakespeare in *A Midsummer Night's Dream*—but he only meant "batlike."

BEARS & BULLS

In the parlance of the stock exchange, a "bear market" declines while a "bull market" rises. The animals are also nicknames for types of investors: a bear typically sells short, anticipating a fall in prices; a bull buys up shares on margin, expecting to sell high before his debt comes due. In other words, the bull is a market optimist and the bear a pessimist.

Some think the original notion was that bears like to grab and pull things down, while bulls toss things up with their horns. But actually we may trace *bear* back to *bear-skins,* 18th-century slang for stock certificates, deriving from the proverb *to sell the bearskin before you've caught the bear.* Besides making some quick cash, the point of this strategy is that you think prices will fall between the time you sell the skin and the time you actually procure it. (And you had better deliver if you value your own skin.) No such colloquialism is available for *bull*; that term probably arose simply by alliteration with "bear."

A SPELLING BEE

Bee is an old Americanism for "busy gathering," drawing again on the notion that bees are the busiest and most social of insects. The metaphor is native to New England, where it originally meant "neighbors united for a purpose." Our earliest printed example is a scintillating news item in the *Boston Gazette* (1769): "Last Thursday about twenty young Ladies met at the house of Mr. L. on purpose for a Spinning Match (or what is called in the Country a Bee)."

The solitary word was confined to the northeast, though various compounds are known across the country. There are spelling bees of course—neighbors gathered to humiliate their young—and quilting bees. We've also heard tell of "apple bees" (for cutting and drying the fruit) and "husking bees" (an especially fun time with corn). Further west, pioneers took up such occupations as "hanging bees" and "lynching bees." Harder to figure is what went on at "shouting bees" and "squirrel bees."

A BUGBEAR

Bugbear and *bogeyman* probably both derive from the same source: the Welsh term *bwg*, "ghost, hobgoblin." *Bug* (originally *bugge*) is the closest English could come to *bwg*, and in fact it first meant "evil spirit" or "scary thing" rather than "insect." Sir Thomas More, for example, warned in 1529 against "such black bugs ... as folk call devils."

Bugbear is merely an improvement on this sense of *bug*; appearing by the 1580s, it is defined by *The Oxford English Dictionary* as "a sort of hobgoblin (presumably in the shape of a bear) supposed to devour naughty children." Thus its current meaning, "object of dread."

As for why we call insects "bugs," it may have to do with the fact that so many of them are so revolting. In any case, this sense doesn't appear before the 1620s, and it may also draw on the Middle English term *budde,* "beetle."

BULLPEN

Readers who remember our former pastime of baseball will be familiar with *bullpen*, the outfield area where pitchers warm up. The word goes back to cattle ranching in the U.S. in the early 1800s, when a bullpen was actually a pen for bulls. Needless to say these pens were crowded and uncomfortable, making a nice metaphor for prisons, dorms, and other stifling enclosures.

It's not clear why baseball adopted the term, around 1920. The most amusing theory—the only real theory, really—traces the expression to big billboards, looming over the warm-up area off left field at many early ballparks, advertising Bull Durham tobacco. These colorful

ads naturally featured a huge bull, who became a sort of mascot to the relievers who tossed the pineapple in the billboard's shadow. It didn't take much thought to link *bull* to the old term *bullpen,* and thus the metaphor was born. Or so the story goes, but it might be just a load of bull.

BULLDOZER

What does a sleeping cow have to do with machinery of destruction? Nothing at all, since the *doze* of *bulldozer* is actually a corruption of the word *dose*. The original expression was *bull-dose,* meaning a dose of lashes applied to recalcitrant cattle with a bullwhip.

Unfortunately, oxen weren't the only victims. In the aftermath of the Civil War, some enemies of Reconstruction (especially in Louisiana) threatened freed slaves with "a dose of the bull" if they dared vote Republican, or even vote at all. And so *to bulldose* or *bulldoze* came by to mean "intimidate with violence," and a *bulldozer* was a big bully.

Somebody thought this would be a good name for the 1920s invention that ripped up ground in a particularly violent and unstoppable fashion. The idea seems to be that these tractors do to the ground what human bulldozers did to blacks. This use traces to the U.S. government's famous 1930 pamphlet, *Water Works & Sewage.*

A CANARD

Once upon a time *canard* was just French for "duck." It's still a duck, but also (in English as in French) a hoax, especially one that people should know better than to swallow. This usage has nothing to do with the perceived intelligence of ducks, but rather with a particular shaggy-duck story.

According to my sources, a fellow named Norbert Cornelissen set about to gauge the gullibility of the French public, and to this end he reported to the press a tale of twenty ducks. He claimed that he took one of his twenty ducks, killed it, and fed it to the remaining nineteen. They quickly gobbled down their former compatriot, at which point Cornelissen took one of the nineteen, killed it, and fed it to the remaining eighteen. Short work was also made of this specimen. Proceeding along, Cornelissen killed each of the remaining ducks in turn, feeding it to the rest, until the last remaining duck had eaten the next-to-last remaining duck. So, Cornelissen bragged, he had fed nineteen ducks to one in very short order.

For some reason, the public was fascinated with this tale and swallowed it whole—the hoax was thus just like a dead duck, or *canard.* And so the term gained currency in France, spreading by the 19th century to England. At first it applied pretty strictly to newspaper hoaxes, but today the term may be used for any unlikely story.

Another source traces this modified meaning to the French saying *vendre des canards à moitié*, "to sell ducks halfway," a cute way of saying "to not sell what you promised." And thus the phrase originally meant "swindle" more than "hoax," though the definitions do overlap.

A COCKTAIL

"The etymology of *cocktail*," wrote H. L. Mencken, "has long engaged the learned, but without persuasive results." For example, in his article "Cock Fighting Today" (1929), William H. Nugent claims that the original term was actually *cock-bread ale*, for a disgusting mixture of stale beer, wine, hard liquor, seeds, roots, leaves, and the kitchen sink. This strange brew was combined with flour to make "cock-bread," which British trainers fed to cocks to put them in a fighting mood. In time, Nugent goes on, *cock-bread ale* was shortened to *cock ale* or simply *cockail*; by the time the term made it to the States (circa 1800), a *t* had "somehow … got into the mixture."

Half a book could be devoted to the other half-cocked theories, for example that an Aztec princess named Xochitl concocted the first cocktail, or that the word derives from the French *coquetier*, "egg cup." But I have to leave room for other cockamamie etymologies.

A COON'S AGE

This is the American version of what began in England as *in a crow's age*. Besides alliterative names, the animals have nothing in common except that they don't live nearly as long as people once thought. Raccoons, who last longer than crows, make it to the age of twelve if they're lucky.

Anyway, *a coon's age* surfaced around the 1840s as an expression for "a real long time," especially as embodied in the still-familiar saying *in a coon's age*. Familiar, but falling off the idiomatic map, as *coon* also has racist connotations. But the slur for "African" has nothing to do with raccoons; rather, the term derives from the Portuguese *barracoos*, "slave pen."

A GONE COON

"I must think of something else as I lie awake," wrote an insomniac Charles Dickens, "or, like that sagacious animal in the United States who recognized the colonel who was such a dead shot, I am a gone coon."

Perhaps Dickens's readers knew what he was talking about, but today the reference is puzzling. Luckily, a little digging through the library reveals his source, apparently the 1839 diary of an English captain named Marryat. In Marryat's version, the sharpshooter is anoth-

er captain rather than a colonel, Captain Martin Scott
from Vermont. Scott was so handy with a rifle that the
local critters knew to avoid him, though they weren't
always successful.

A case in point involves a raccoon who attempted to
hide from the captain high in a tree. Scott spotted it anyway and raised his gun, at which point the animal began
stalling. Here's Marryat's account:

"I beg your pardon mister," said the raccoon, very
politely, "but may I ask if your name is Scott?"

"Yes," replied the captain.

"*Martin* Scott?" continued the raccoon.

"Yes," replied the captain.

"*Captain* Martin Scott?" still continued the animal.

"Yes," replied the captain; "Captain Martin Scott."

"Oh then," says the animal, "I may just as well come
down, for I'm a gone coon."

Yes, this was once considered a laugh riot, even by
the likes of Dickens. It's possible, though, that Marryat's
source was an actual incident from the Revolutionary War.

As this tale goes, a Yankee scout attempted to spy on
a British encampment by donning a raccoon skin and
climbing a tree over the camp. But a sharp-eyed Brit
spotted him, taking him for an exceptionally large coon,
and thus an inviting target. But when the Englishman
raised his rifle, the American cried out, "Hold on! If you
won't shoot, I'll come down. I am a gone coon!" So star-

tled was the redcoat to hear a raccoon talk that he dropped his gun and fled.

In some parts of the country, *a gone goose* is more familiar than *gone coon,* and in fact the former expression saw print earlier, in 1830. This seems to have been a saying peculiar to New England; New Yorkers would say "a gone gander."

A LAME DUCK

Coined by 1760, *lame duck* was originally English slang for a defaulter on the stock exchange, and then more generally for a bad credit risk. "I'll have no lame duck's daughter in my family," huffs a forbidding parent in Thackeray's *Vanity Fair* (1848). The point seems to be that the crippled "duck" is (like the animal) shunned by the healthier ducks, who have things to do and places to fly without being dragged down by lamesters.

But as it crossed the Atlantic, *lame duck* dropped this sense into the drink and took on the meaning "a crippled politician." The *Congressional Globe* of 14 January 1863, for example, refers to a "receptacle of 'lame ducks' or broken-down politicians," which actually makes more sense than the British version. All a lame duck can really do (besides cause spiteful mischief) is wait to die, which most people agree doesn't happen soon enough in politicians' cases.

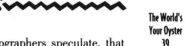

It's possible, as some lexicographers speculate, that the American *lame duck* never had anything to do with the English saying. Rather, perhaps, it was based on the older epithet *dead duck*, as in *Don't waste powder on a dead duck.* (Andrew Jackson, for example, had used the expression "political dead duck" in an 1844 missive.) Though a politician would be "dead" in March, he was only "lame" until then—if he wasn't lame his whole term, that is.

AN UGLY DUCKLING

As everyone knows, the ugly duckling of Hans Christian Andersen's tale, mocked by all, grows up to be a swan—far more beautiful than any lousy duck. The theme is the old one of the misplaced child, and the moral the old notion that you can't tell a diamond from the rough. In other words, what is strange or unpleasant at the start may turn out brilliant or beautiful when mature, while what is beautiful from the beginning may, like a flower that blooms too soon, decay faster with time. The prom queen is not often still stunning in adulthood; the slow-seeming child may be like those still waters that run deep. And that's your fill of clichés for the day.

A WHITE ELEPHANT

This clever expression for "a big useless expensive object" comes to us from Thailand. In olden times, whenever a rare albino elephant was born or captured it would immediately be consecrated to the Siamese emperor, who was known as "Lord of the White Elephant."

Now, nobody could ride a white elephant but the emperor, nor could anyone dispose of one without his consent. So if a particular courtier or aristocrat got under the emperor's skin, he would be graced with the "gift" of a sacred white elephant. The victim couldn't ride the thing, or do anything else but feed and maintain it, which as you can imagine was a costly enterprise.

Not to be outdone, Americans came up with a native explanation for the phrase, though it's of dubious authenticity. According to the *Morris Dictionary of Word and Phrase Origins*, in the early days of the circus a certain company got hold of one of these rare Siamese albinos, which became an instant hit. The famed showman P. T. Barnum retaliated by taking one of his own elephants, whitewashing it, and launching an advertising blitz.

With the novelty of the true article destroyed, Barnum triumphed, and his competitor was stuck with an attraction that cost more to house and feed than it was worth. He couldn't even sell the thing, in a market Barnum dominated, so the white elephant turned into a white elephant.

A FINE KETTLE OF FISH

The best *The Oxford English Dictionary* can do with this
one is to point out the irony: a fine (or pretty) kettle of fish
is neither fine nor pretty (nor a kettle), it's a total mess.

Literal kettles of fish were staples of toney river pic-
nics in the later 18th century; "It is customary," noted
Thomas Newte in 1791, "for the gentlemen who live near
the Tweed to entertain their neighbours and friends with
a Fete Champetre [outdoor feast], which they call giving
'a kettle of fish.' Tents or marquees are pitched near the
flowery bands of the river,... a fire is kindled, and live
salmon are thrown into boiling kettles."

But this charming spectacle couldn't be what our
phrase refers to, since *pretty kettle of fish* (as in "fiasco")
predates Newte's work by about 50 years. It's possible
that the "kettle" in this phrase isn't really a kettle in the
sense of the Old English word *cetel,* "cauldron," but
something else.

One theory is that *kettle* is an abbreviation of *kettle-
net,* a term of lost origin for fishing nets used to bag
mackerel. One can imagine the toil and confusion of the
fish as they're pulled onto the boat in their "kettle." The
problem is that *kettle-net* isn't found written until 1881.
On the other hand, something called a *kiddelus,* which
may amount to the same device, *is* mentioned in the
Magna Carta.

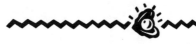
Yet another possibility is that *kettle* here isn't *cetel* but rather a form of the Scottish word *kittle*, "to confuse." Or perhaps, as William Walsh suggests in his *Handy-Book of Literary Curiosities,* the phrase "was used in derision by some early Saxon cook who, having overbroiled his fish, spoiled his whole *cetel*-ful."

NEITHER FISH NOR FOWL

In its original form this phrase went more like *neither fish nor flesh nor a good red herring.* Apparently the reference is to eating these things; the English clergy ate lots of fish while laborers preferred "flesh" (meat and poultry), while nobody but beggars bothered with red herring. (The aristocracy ate what they pleased.)

So something that was neither fish nor flesh nor a good red herring was effectively nothing at all, stomach-wise. Eventually *red herring* dropped from the saying, probably once people realized that herring *is* a fish. *Flesh* then gave way to *fowl* as the former dropped out of use as a synonym for *meat.*

It's also possible, as Charles Funk theorizes, that the phrase dates to the time of Henry VIII

and refers to the Church of England's split with Rome.
(The first printed citation *is* from that time.) "One who
abstained from neither fish nor flesh when days of fasting
were prescribed," Funk says, "were [*sic*] neither Roman
Catholic nor Dissenters, neither one thing nor the
other—just plain irreligious." This doesn't explain *good
red herring*, but that may not really have been part of the
original phrase.

- **See also:** *red herring* (page 46).

SPANISH FLY

Besides producing a "love potion" of dubious value, the
Spanish fly isn't even a fly—it's a beetle.

Found not just in Spain but all over Europe, the insect
gets its reputation from *cantharidin*, a nasty chemical
that seethes through its body. This is the stuff usually
called "Spanish fly," and you're advised to avoid it: it's
poisonous. In fact, just getting a bit on your skin will
cause blisters, which is why American relatives of the
bug are called "blister beetles."

Despite the chemical's unpleasant effects, it's been
used for centuries (in very moderate doses) as a love
drug. It's a diuretic for sure, but whether it's more stimu-
lating than that is uncertain. The idea is no doubt due to
such romantic associations as rashes with love—that
love can make you ill is a very, very old idea.

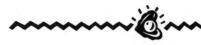

TO GET YOUR GOAT

An old belief in racing circles is that goats are good medicine for a jittery thoroughbred. The superstition was taken pretty seriously in the 19th century, when trainers regularly kept goat companions in their stables. It was also taken seriously by rivals and gamblers, who on the night before a big race would attempt to "get the goat," that is, to steal it. This was supposed to irritate or dismay the horse and thus cause it to lose.

Whether this is really the origin of *to get one's goat* (meaning "to peeve") is debatable. The expression doesn't show up in print before Jack London wrote it in a 1910 letter and then in his novel *Smoke Bellew* (1912), and he wasn't referring to the races. H. L. Mencken reports the racetrack origin in his *American Language*, but remains somewhat agnostic.

A WILD-GOOSE CHASE

So far as I know, nobody's ever caught a wild goose by chasing it, which many presume is the point of this phrase. At least Samuel Johnson did in his 1755 dictionary. But when it was coined, in the late 16th century, it wasn't the goose's elusiveness that mattered so much as its flight patterns.

In particular, a "wild-goose chase" was a horse race in

which the leader could go wherever he chose, and the other contestants had to follow closely. The result was, to the imaginative eye, much like the flight of wild geese, who follow their leader no matter how erratic his course.

This explains the earliest surviving use of the phrase, found in Shakespeare's *Romeo and Juliet* (act 2, scene 4). The voluble Mercutio, after trading a series of witty

remarks with his friend Romeo, likens their banter to a "wild-goose chase," which he intends as flattery: Romeo is outmaneuvering and exhausting him.

Wild-goose chases of the horsey sort were but a passing fad, and so it makes sense that people would forget the reference though they remembered the metaphor. In time, the sense "exhausting, erratic chase" gave way to "pointless chase," which was part of the original meaning anyway. However, to use *wild-goose chase* to mean "pursuit of an imaginary or non-existent goal" is just wrong.

A RED HERRING

If anything smells more powerful than a herring, it's a red (that is, a smoked) herring. Which makes it ideal for training hunting dogs to follow a scent—sometimes you have to start them out with something less subtle than the odor of dead cat.

In case you think I jest, once upon a time hunters actually dragged red herrings over the ground to train their pooches; the smell, I'm told, lingers for quite some time. In fact, it obliterates just about any other scent, say that of a fox on the run. Competing fox hunters also took advantage of this technique in a maneuver known as "faulting the hounds."

Likewise, red herring is very effective at concealing the scent of an escaping thief, and clever crooks of the 17th century would foil pursuant bloodhounds by dragging a red herring behind them for a while and then dropping it. Once the dog got a snoutful of that, the only thing it was going to track down was the discarded fish.

Whether from fox hunting or cop evading, there arose at about this time the saying *to drag a red herring across the trail,* meaning "to send out false or misleading signals." The abbreviated *red herring* appears by the 1880s.

A DARK HORSE

Though now used for unlikely political candidates and other longshots, *dark horse* originally (and not surprisingly) referred to racehorses. The *dark* part had nothing to do with the color of the horse's coat; rather, it means "unknown" and derives from the practice of training a race horse in secrecy, therefore keeping its powers and weaknesses "in the dark." (Jockeys were wont to say, "the dark horse will win the race.")

Players of the political horse race lost little time adapting this phrase, which first appeared in 1831, to their own uses. It became a metaphor for "someone unexpectedly drafted as a candidate from the sidelines of a political convention, usually because none of the declared candidates is deemed acceptable." Obviously, *dark horse* is a lot more concise.

The first human dark horse was James Polk, who wasn't even considered a presidential candidate until the eighth ballot of the 1844 Democratic Convention. He went on to win the election, despite his unofficial campaign slogan, "Who's Polk?" From even farther behind, Franklin Pierce charged into the nomination on the 49th ballot of the 1852 Democratic Convention (he wasn't even in the race until the 35th). According to William Safire, the Democrats' winning slogan that year was the inspired "We Polked You in 1844; We'll Pierce You in 1852." The political use of *dark horse* seems to date to after the Polking but before the Piercing.

A HOBBYHORSE

"He's riding that old hobbyhorse again," you might say of someone's *idée fixe*. The term of course derives from those wooden toy ponies children once got for Christmas and rode, and rode, and rode until something new caught their attention.

What you may not know is that *hobbyhorse* means "horse-horse," more or less; *hobby* originally signified "small Irish horse." But by the 16th century this meaning had been forgotten and the redundant compound became the regular name for sticks with wooden horse-heads. (The more elaborate rocking horse wasn't invented for several more centuries.)

Children's fixation on these toys inspired the condescending metaphor of *hobbyhorse* for a trivial pursuit. The *-horse* half was dropped in the 19th century, thus bringing the term full circle to *hobby*, no longer redundant but no longer having any link to its original sense.

A MARE'S NEST

Of course horses don't build nests; that's the point of this phrase. *Mare's nest* originally referred (circa 1600) to a big discovery that turned out to be an illusion or a fraud. Perhaps someone once actually claimed to have discovered a mare's nest, or the phrase may always have been metaphorical. In either case, it gradually came to mean simply "deception," and more recently (for some reason) "complicated mess."

This last meaning may suggest a connection to *nightmare,* but in fact that word has nothing to do with horses, except in some people's imaginations. The *mare* of nightmare is the Anglo-Saxon word for "incubus," a nasty sort of male spirit which lies on, or with, women as they sleep.

MONKEY BUSINESS

This metaphor for mischief was coined in the early 1800s, around the time zoos started sprouting up in Europe and people got their first look at actual monkeys. Like countless other simian similes (*monkey around, you little monkey, monkeyshines, a barrel of monkeys,* etc.), this is based on the little primates' famous penchant for mimicry, meddling, and foolishness. Considerably older is the Chinese saying *You have a full thousand monkeytricks!*

On the other hand is the say-

ing *to make a monkey out of,* in which the animal is the victim rather than the perpetrator of mockery. It dates to the 17th century, when taunting and tormenting monkeys was a popular carnival attraction.

In case you're curious about what *monkeyshines* means, *shines* was a common word in 19th-century America for "tricks."

THE WORLD'S MY OYSTER

This smug little saying goes back to Shakespeare, and to his generally insufferable character Pistol in *The Merry Wives of Windsor* (circa 1597).

The situation: Pistol is hitting up Sir John Falstaff, the lovable butt of the play, for some cash; "I will not lend thee a penny," Falstaff replies. "Why then," Pistol retorts, "the world's mine oyster, / Which I with sword will open." In other words, if Pistol can't borrow he's going to steal, using his sword to pry open victims' purses and snatch their pearls.

Though Pistol's mostly a braggart, he's probably talking turkey. But his thievish and threatening intentions have been forgotten today, as we use the phrase as a conceited proclamation that the world's riches are available for our plucking.

TO PIGEONHOLE

Though they were once more common, you still occasionally see buildings or walls lined with pigeon houses or "dovecotes" (pigeons are closely related to doves). The pigeon townhouses have small entry holes, naturally enough called *pigeonholes.*

But it's the houses and not the holes that lie behind the metaphor, which originally referred (in the 17th century) to small boxes or compartments in a desk, sometimes arranged in rows, like cotes. Later the verb *to pigeonhole* was coined for the act of stuffing things into these crannies, which are seldom spacious enough for the trick, though small enough to be ignored when possible. And thus the current sense of *pigeonhole,* to stuff a person or notion into a well-defined but ill-fitting category.

PORK BARREL

"Pork-barrel politics" has long been a favorite cry of legislators who oppose wasteful public spending (in districts other than their own). The origins of "pork barrel" are misty, but professional pundit William Safire thinks it probable the phrase derives "from the pre-Civil War practice of periodically distributing salt pork to the slaves from huge barrels." He quotes an article from a 1919 issue of the *National Municipal Review*:

Oftentimes the eagerness of the slaves would result in a rush upon the pork barrel, in which each would strive to grab as much as possible for himself. Members of Congress in the stampede to get their local appropriation items into the omnibus river and harbor bills behaved so much like Negro slaves rushing the pork barrel, that these bills were facetiously styled "pork barrel" bills, and the system which originated them has thus become known as the pork-barrel system.

The term *pork barrel* in this sense dates more or less to the 1860s, and the shorthand term *pork* to the next decade. In an 1879 issue of the *Congressional Record*, we may read that "St. Louis is going to have some of the 'pork' indirectly, but it will not do any good."

A more recently coinage is the gerund "pork-barreling," which first shows up in a 1967 issue of the English magazine the *Economist*. "The one piece of regional pork-barrelling at last week's Labour party conference," this sober journal intoned, "was the Prime Minister's promise that two aluminum smelters, using subsidised electricity, would be built, probably in development areas." Another valuable American export.

YOU CAN'T MAKE A SILK PURSE FROM A SOW'S EAR

It's anybody's guess who first thought of this clever metaphor for trying to make something fine out of coarse materials. A French-English dictionary of 1611 cites as an old saying, "A man cannot make a cheverill purse of a sow's ear" (*cheverill* is kid leather). Many versions of the phrase circulated in the 17th century, some involving velvet caps, others satin or velvet purses. We arrive at *silk purse* and the now familiar form only in 1738 with Swift's *Polite Conversation,* also the first written source of *raining cats and dogs* (see page 96).

Though the literal sense of the phrase is hardly disputable, someone did recently try to prove it wrong by interweaving silk fibers with hairs from a pig's ear. I wish I had so much time on my hands.

WELSH RABBIT

Welsh rabbit is *not* a corruption of *Welsh rarebit,* as many people think. Just the opposite is true: *rarebit* is an attempt to gussy up the more disparaging term, whose point is that the Welsh treat toasted cheese as a sort of game dish. (The English have a tradition of such insults: sheep's-head stew was once called "German duck"; red herring, "Norfolk capons"; potatoes, "Irish apricots";

shrimp, "Gravesend sweetmeats"; etc.)

On the origin of *rarebit*, William Walsh observes:

> Coming across the word Welsh rabbit, [an amateur etymologist] gazed through solemn spectacles at this mare's nest, and decided that a bit of toasted cheese could not by any stretch of the imagination be considered a game animal, but it might well be a rare bit. So he jumped at the conclusion that time, and the corruptions which time effects, must have done their work on this word, and decided to restore its original beauty and significance.

Au contraire, Walsh argues; the real answer is that Welshmen really are fond of toasted cheese. (In other words, he thinks the slur is deserved.) Walsh doesn't name the culprit, but according to *The Oxford English Dictionary* it was Francis Gross, writing in his 1785 *Dictionary of the Vulgar Tongue.*

The origin of the dish seems to trace to the late 17th or early 18th century, when Wales was relatively poor and common folk could hardly afford to eat real rabbit.

A PAPER TIGER

"Political power grows out of the barrel of a gun"; "let a hundred flowers bloom"; "paper tiger"—these are just a few of the catchy phrases that come to us from that noted phrasemaker Mao Tse-tung.

He may have been coining in the first two cases, but he was only quoting in the third: *paper tiger* is an old Chinese metaphor for "hollow threat." But Mao did bring it to the Western world in a 1946 interview when he likened the enemies of Communism to paper tigers whose roar is impressive but whose bite is pathetic. (Mao was almost beaten to the punch by Shakespeare, who uses "empty tiger" in *Romeo and Juliet*.)

Speaking of paper, the expression *paper chase* is also an animalogy of a sort, deriving from a game called "hares and hounds." One side, called the "hares," runs about helter-skelter, scattering pieces of paper behind them, while the other side, the "hounds," attempts to follow the trail and catch the hares before they've reached a goal.

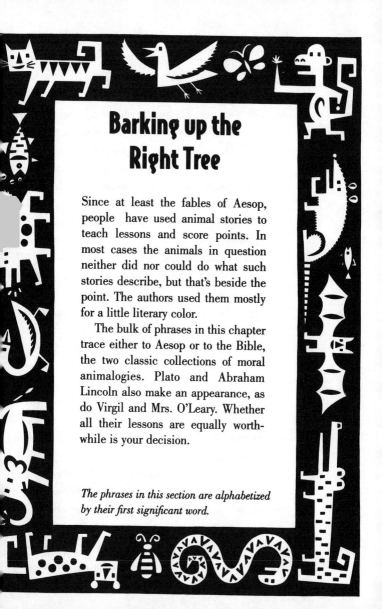

Barking up the Right Tree

Since at least the fables of Aesop, people have used animal stories to teach lessons and score points. In most cases the animals in question neither did nor could do what such stories describe, but that's beside the point. The authors used them mostly for a little literary color.

The bulk of phrases in this chapter trace either to Aesop or to the Bible, the two classic collections of moral animalogies. Plato and Abraham Lincoln also make an appearance, as do Virgil and Mrs. O'Leary. Whether all their lessons are equally worthwhile is your decision.

The phrases in this section are alphabetized by their first significant word.

BEHEMOTH AND LEVIATHAN

Both of these big and nasty beasts are biblical. They rear their heads in the Book of Job, a story about bad things happening to good people. God listens for chapter upon chapter to mortal moaning until He can't take it any more. He finally swoops down to confound the whiners with such humiliating queries as "Where wast thou when I laid the foundations of the earth?" (Job 38:4).

God brags about the terrible grandeur of His creation, which is so far beyond mankind it's frightening. For example: "Behold now behemoth," He cries, "which I made with thee; he eateth grass as an ox. Lo now, his strength is in his loins, and his force is in the navel of his belly" (40:15–16). God also asks some searching questions: "Canst thou draw out leviathan with an hook? or his tongue with a cord which thou lettest down?" Apparently not. "Canst thou put an hook into his nose? or bore through his jaw with a thorn?" Um, no. "Will he make many supplications unto thee? will he speak soft words unto thee?" (41:1–3). I don't think so, but what's "leviathan" anyway?

That's a question people have pondered for centuries. Some literal-minded readers have claimed behemoth and leviathan are actual animals—a hippo or an elephant, for example, in behemoth's case; a crocodile or whale in leviathan's. Scholars sort of agree in the case of behemoth, whose name probably derives from the Egyptian *p'ehe'mau,* "water ox." Leviathan, on the other hand, is more likely a mythical creature. There's a strong family resemblance with Lothan, a seven-headed sea monster found in Canaanite myth, and Typhon, a many-headed dragon in Greek legend. Real or not, these two beasts survive today only as metaphors for huge and fearsome forces.

A BIRD IN THE HAND IS WORTH TWO IN THE BUSH

Tracing the origin of this phrase is like hunting birds in a bush, but tradition grants the coinage to Will Sommers, court jester to King Henry VIII and one of the most famous clowns in English history.

Sommers happened one day to visit the Earl of Surrey, whom he'd done a number of good turns, and spotted a particularly beautiful kingfisher. "The bird is yours," said the gracious lord, and Will pranced off merrily to show the world his new gift.

Now it also happened that the Earl of Northampton had taken a shine to the bird and was disappointed to learn that Surrey had already disposed of it. Hoping to cut a deal, Northampton sent a message to the clown, promising two equally beautiful birds when caught at some later date in return for the kingfisher presently.

"Sirrah," Sommers replied to the messenger, "tell your master that I am much obliged for his liberal offer, but

that I prefer one bird in hand for two in the bush."

Whether Sommers's quip was original (or whether he quipped at all) is open to argument. What we do know is that very similar sayings began cropping up in English proverb books during Henry's reign, one example being "A bird in the hand is worth three in the wood." The granddaddy of all such sayings appears to be Aesop's fable "The Nightingale and the Hawk," in which a hawk tells the nightingale he's just captured that "I would be stupid to give up a bird I have now on the chance of maybe catching a better one later."

A CAMEL THROUGH THE EYE OF A NEEDLE

"And again I say unto you," preaches Jesus in the Gospel according to Saint Matthew (19:24), "It is easier for a camel to go through the eye of a needle, than for a rich man to enter into the kingdom of God." His point is easi-

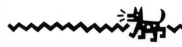
ly grasped, if convenient for some to ignore; but it may not be clear why he picks on camels. Simply put, the animal was the biggest Jesus' audience would ever have seen.

The phrase is a good example of Jesus' penchant for hyperbole (consider his talk of "the beam that is in thine own eye" earlier in Matthew, and his claim that "the very hairs of your head are all numbered"). Mark Twain had a bit of fun with it when he wrote in his notebook that "It is easier for a cannibal to enter the Kingdom of Heaven through the eye of a rich man's needle than it is for any other foreigner to read the terrible German script." Less ironic is one cigarette manufacturer's hyperbolic ad campaign, famous in the 1960s and '70s: "I'd walk a mile for a Camel."

TO CAST PEARLS BEFORE SWINE

Another of Jesus' coinages, this phrase is found in the Sermon on the Mount. "Give not that which is holy unto the dogs," he warns (Matt. 7:6), "neither cast ye pearls before swine, lest they trample them under their feet, and turn again and rend you."

As usual, what Jesus means is arguable, though the image is clear: if you throw something valuable at a rushing pig, the swine isn't likely to stop and admire it. More likely, it will stomp on your pearls and then on you. (Well, probably not, but let's grant the thesis for the moment.)

The real point has something to do with offering pearls of holy wisdom to swinish unbelievers, who will only mock the gift and then persecute the messenger. Who precisely Jesus has in mind is the rub, though it's probably the hated Sadduces and Pharisees, self-proclaimed holy men who had nothing but contempt for Christ's gospel.

A DOG IN THE MANGER

The meaning of this phrase—"someone who refuses to give up what he doesn't need to someone who does"—is pretty perplexing unless you know the story it's based on, one of Aesop's fables. "A dog was lying in a manger," reads one anonymous translation, "on the hay which had been put there for the oxen, and when they came and tried to eat, he growled and snapped at them and wouldn't let them get at their food. 'What a selfish beast,' said one of them to his companions; 'he can't eat himself and yet he won't let those eat who can.'" Not a very dramatic story perhaps (one waits in vain for the dog to get his reward), but one that has, out of the many Aesopian fables enshrined in English phrase, lent us one of the more interesting sayings.

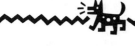

DON'T CHANGE HORSES IN MIDSTREAM

Every source gives a different account of exactly what President Abraham Lincoln said on June 9, 1864, but they all agree that in some form or other he coined this phrase on that date. According to some, Lincoln cited the "story of an old Dutch farmer," which would mean the saying was already known, if not a cliché. Others put it directly in the horse's mouth.

Either way, Lincoln was replying to the National Union League, a Yankee political group who sent congratulations on his renomination to the presidency. Lincoln was characteristically modest; in the version recorded in *Bartlett's Familiar Quotations,* he said,

> I do not allow myself to suppose that either the convention or the League have concluded to decide that I am either the greatest or best man in America, but rather they have concluded that it is not best to swap horses while crossing the river, and have further concluded that I am not so poor a horse that they might not make a botch of it in trying to swap.

More concisely, what Lincoln meant was that it's best to ride the horse you came in on, because changing in the middle of the ride is likely to leave you all wet.

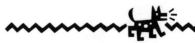

DON'T COUNT YOUR CHICKENS BEFORE THEY'RE HATCHED

These words of wisdom hatched from one of Aesop's fables, "The Milkmaid and Her Pail." A farmer's daughter is daydreaming as she returns to the dairy with a pail of fresh milk on her head. "The milk in this pail will provide me with cream," she imagines, "which I'll make into butter and sell at the market. I'll use the money I make to buy lots of eggs, and when these hatch I'll have a fine flock of chickens."

Her dreams don't stop there. The chickens will earn her money for a gown, and the gown will win her the attention of the young fellows of the village. She delights in imagining how fine and haughty a figure she'll cut; "I shall toss my head and have nothing to say to them," she thinks.

But obviously she's counted her chickens before they're hatched. Carried away in her flight of fancy, she tosses her head at the imagined crowd of suitors, and off flies the pail of milk. Thus ends another brilliant career.

DON'T LOOK A GIFT HORSE IN THE MOUTH

Why would anybody want to look a horse in the mouth, gift or not? Because by examining its teeth, you can get a pretty good idea how old it is, a fact of particular interest to horse traders.

But examining a *gift* horse this way is obviously rude, even if you suspect the animal's older (and more decrepit) than advertised. The same goes for complaining about the defects of any gift, which was called "looking a gift horse in the mouth" at least as far back as A.D. 420, when Saint Jerome quoted it as a proverb. Most European languages have a version; the original English saying was "don't look a given horse in the mouth."

A much more recent coinage is *straight from the horse's mouth,* which also refers to the truth's lying in the teeth. Though it may go as far back as the 1830s, it passed into popular parlance only in the 1920s, a heyday of horse racing and probably of unscrupulous horse dealing as well. The phrase was first published in a 1928 story by P. G. Wodehouse, who knew a thing or two about thoroughbreds. "The prospect of getting the true facts—straight, as it were, from the horse's mouth—held him fascinated."

TO EAT CROW

I'm told that crow is rather untasty; frankly, I don't want to find out. If true, it's sufficient to explain this phrase, meaning "to be forced to do something unpleasant," especially eating one's words. This makes even better sense since *to crow* has since the 1500s meant "boast" or "rub one's achievements in others' faces." Therefore, *to eat crow* is to swallow your own boasts.

Pure logic aside, there are also a few amusing etymologies for *eating crow*. The first is a tale of a penny-pinching American boardinghouse keeper and his disgruntled boarder, who was wont to complain about the miserly and unpalatable fare. These complaints the host repeatedly brushed off as "too partikler," proclaiming that he (a manly man) could eat anything—crow, for example. Tiring of such boasts, the boarder resolved to put his host to the test. He shot a big fat crow and got the cook to prepare it with a special seasoning of snuff. At dinner he presented the resultant dish with the challenge, "Now, my dear sir, you have said a thousand times, if you have said it once, that you can eat crow; here is one very carefully cooked." The keeper had no choice but to dig in, downing two bites before rushing off to be sick. "I've et crow," he cried, "but dang me if I hanker arter it."

The second story concerns an encounter, during the American Civil War, of a Union private with a Southern planter. The private had shot a tame crow on the planter's property and was caught red-handed by the owner. The planter seized the private's gun, pointed it at him, and demanded that he eat the crow he'd killed. The private ate his meal without much complaint, save to say that he didn't exactly "hanker after" crow.

This was good enough for the planter, who handed back the gun and ordered the soldier off his property. But the private had other plans; he aimed his gun at the

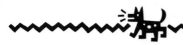

planter and said, "Now you've got to eat your share of crow." The next day, the planter brought a complaint to the soldier's commander, who had ordered his men to leave civilians be. When the private was brought forth, the commander asked, "Have you seen this gentleman before?" The private replied, "Yes, I believe we dined together yesterday."

A FLY IN THE OINTMENT

This is one of the less biblical-sounding biblical phrases, from the wisdom book of Ecclesiastes. "Dead flies cause the ointment ... to send forth a stinking savour," he writes; "so doth a little folly him that is in reputation for wisdom and honour" (10:1).

Put in plain English, the more perfect you are, the more offensive ("stinking") your follies will appear. But if that's the case, I don't know whether it argues more against follies or reputation. Perhaps it's better to let people underestimate you rather than to find yourself emitting stinking savours when you slip.

In any case, this piece of wisdom has become, minus the "dead" part, less consequential every century. Today the fly in the ointment is more likely a sour note or tiny smudge than a character flaw.

TO KILL THE GOOSE THAT LAYS THE GOLDEN EGGS

That stupid greed has been around practically forever is proved by this fable, which is about 2,500 years old and already that vice's perfect epitome.

Aesop doesn't bother to explain where the goose came from, or how it managed to lay eggs of gold. What matters is that a certain greedy couple had it, and that eventually they began plotting how to do better than just one golden egg per day. "Imagining the bird must be made of gold inside," the fable relates, "they decided to kill it to secure the whole store of precious metal at once."

Of course, there was no precious metal inside the goose. Like many bad businessmen, the greedy couple didn't understand that wealth is something produced rather than preexistent—something that comes from careful nurturing rather than a quick killing.

A LEOPARD CAN'T CHANGE ITS SPOTS

In the middle of the harangue that gives us the word *jeremiad,* the prophet Jeremiah pauses to ask, "Can the Ethiopian change his skin, or the leopard his spots?" The tacit answer to this rhetorical question sets up Jeremiah's punch line: "then may ye also do good, that are accustomed to evil" (Jer. 13:23).

The prophet is fingering a bunch of sinful and self-righteous Jews, who presume to object when God justly metes out their punishment. Jeremiah has news for them: worse is coming, and you've got no hope. You are too complacent in your evil, too blind to your sin, and it's too late for you to change—it would be like a leopard trying to change its spots. One wonders, though, why Jeremiah's bothering with them at all if their fate is sealed.

MRS. O'LEARY'S COW

The most infamous bovine in American history, Mrs. O'Leary's cow has borne the blame for the disastrous Chicago fire of 1871. But the actual truth is another issue—everyone involved told a different story, a lot of the claims were speculative, and there's a good chance the poor beast was framed.

But let's begin at the beginning. The scene is 137 De Koven Street, Chicago; the date, October 8; the time, 8:30 P.M. Mrs. O'Leary, afflicted with a sore foot, has retired to bed. Next door, fiddle player Pat McLaughlin is throwing a bash, the highlight of which, besides alcohol, is oysters. Now various of McLaughlin's guests get the idea in their heads to stew these oysters in fresh milk. And guess where they go looking?

A mass expedition to O'Leary's barn leaves the guest of honor, namely the cow, less than flattered. In fact she took powerful exception to being milked by strangers and retaliated by kicking a candle into a pile of shavings. The rest is history.

There are other versions of the tale, which is not surprising. McLaughlin & Co. later denied the whole business, oyster stew and all. Some people suggested that the cow kicked over a lantern because she hadn't been milked at all that evening. Others speculated that Mrs. O'Leary herself deliberately set the blaze because she was mad about something or other. But I like the one about stewed oysters.

A SCAPEGOAT

Another biblical coinage, *scapegoat* is actually a mistranslation from the Hebrew. When William Tyndale Englished the Pentateuch in 1530, a certain passage from the Book of Leviticus confused him. Describing rituals to be observed on the solemn Jewish holiday Yom Kippur, the author of Leviticus refers to an animal sacrifice involving two goats. One goat was doomed by a lottery to slaughter, while the other—bearing the community's sins—was let to escape into the desert "for Azazel."

Tyndale couldn't make heads or tails out of *Azazel*. So, taking a cue from the standard Latin translation, he just pretended it was an obscure name for the escaped goat itself—or, to use the common Renaissance abbreviation, the "scaped goat." Thus his translation: "The goat, on which the lot fell to be the scapegoat, shall be presented

alive before the LORD, to make an atonement with him, and to let him go for a scapegoat into the wilderness" (Lev. 16:10).

The point's clear: this "scapegoat" would meet the LORD in the desert and pay there for the entire community's sinfulness. Thus our current use of the term. But in the Hebrew the goat meets not God, but Azazel, from the Hebrew for "angry god." Scholars now agree that Azazel was some sort of evil demon, though he, she, or it is never again mentioned in the Bible.

TO SEPARATE SHEEP FROM GOATS

Knowing his time is nigh, Jesus comforts his disciples by describing the glorious day when he shall return with angels and gather all nations around him for judgment. "And he shall separate them one from another, as a shepherd divideth his sheep from the goats: And he shall set the sheep on his right hand, but the goats on the left" (Matt. 25:32–33).

Jesus is referring to a practice that still survives in Palestine. Even though sheep and goats pasture together just fine, they don't get along while moving. So when a shepherd needs to transport both sheep and goats to another locale, he divides them first.

Certainly, if I were a sheep I'd be mighty glad to be separated from the goats, who symbolize the damned and who are destined, after the Final Judgment, to wind up in "everlasting fire, prepared for the devil and his angels" (25:41). Why sheep get to be the good guys and goats the bad guys is probably due to the fact that wool was a lot more valuable than goatskin.

This blatant discrimination against goats survives even in today's usage, while only a hint of brimstone remains. We metaphorically separate sheep and goats now only to mete out congratulations and ridicule, critical rather than literal salvation and damnation.

A SNAKE IN THE GRASS

This phrase has a venerable history, tracing to the poetry of Virgil. To be exact, it's found in his third eclogue, a poetizing contest between two shepherds, each of whom claims to be the more beloved by his fellows, and each of whom also claims to be the more torn up by passion.

The pathos mounts as the two go back and forth, trading boasts and complaints, until one, Damoetas, proclaims, "May you who gather flowers and strawberries from the ground, /Flee, you children, from the cold snake hiding in the grass." This line doesn't come out of nowhere; Virgil seems to have particular "children" and a particular "snake" in mind. Who they are doesn't really matter much; the point is that while love (like flowers and strawberries) is beautiful and sweet, it is also full of danger (snakes).

TO STRAIN AT A GNAT

Strain at a gnat is a mistranslation of what reads in the original Greek as "strain *out* a gnat." Even the original doesn't make much sense unless you're acquainted with the Mosaic law as embodied in the Book of Leviticus. There we find this injunction: "And every creeping thing that creepeth upon the earth shall be an abomination; it shall not be eaten" (11:14).

In New Testament times strictly observant Jews applied this law by always straining their wine before drinking it, lest gnats or any creeping things had got into the wineskin. Especial sticklers for this and other dietary regulations were the scribes and Pharisees, literal-minded and orthodox sorts who could strain out gnats but not avoid the taunts of Jesus. "Woe unto you, scribes and Pharisees, hypocrites!" shouts Jesus in the Gospels. "Ye blind guides, which strain at a gnat, and swallow a camel" (Matt. 23:23–24).

We know the King James translators goofed on *at/out*, but they got "swallow a camel" right. The point of this rather gross image is that the super-holy scribes and Pharisees make a big deal out of trivial laws like this while figuratively swallowing camels, that is, tolerating gross behavior that violates the spirit if not the letter of the Torah.

A SWAN SONG

The first "swan song" was sung by Socrates in Plato's dialogue *Phaedo* (fourth century B.C.). Condemned to death by an Athenian jury on charges of immorality and heresy, Socrates welcomes his fatal cup of hemlock.

Why? Because he is drawing closer to a meeting with his immortal patron, the god Apollo, divine philosopher.

So his friends shouldn't be surprised if he "sings" merrily about his doom, which to him will be a release from the
petty cares of mortal existence.

For Socrates is like the swan, another of Apollo's
favored creatures. Men had observed that when facing
death the swan will cry loudly and long; they thought this
was out of fear, since they themselves fear death. Wrong,
Socrates says; swans, "having sung all their life long, do
then sing more, and more sweetly, than ever, rejoicing in
the thought that they are about to go away to Apollo,
whose ministers they are."

This fanciful notion inspired much folklore and lent us
our cliché for one's last and theoretically best perfor-
mance. The idea was faithfully put forth by Aristotle,
Cicero, Chaucer, Shakespeare, and many other brilliant
writers. But of course swans don't really sing; at best,
they honk.

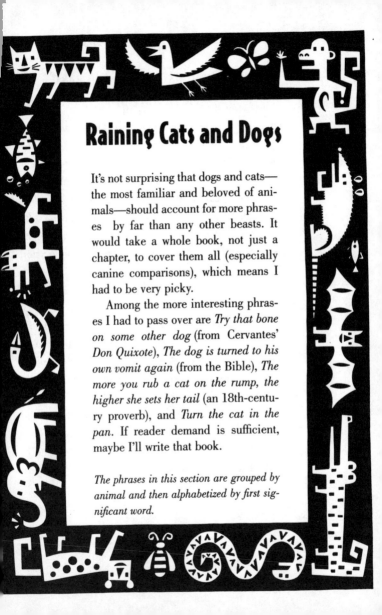

Raining Cats and Dogs

It's not surprising that dogs and cats—
the most familiar and beloved of animals—should account for more phrases by far than any other beasts. It
would take a whole book, not just a
chapter, to cover them all (especially
canine comparisons), which means I
had to be very picky.

Among the more interesting phrases I had to pass over are *Try that bone
on some other dog* (from Cervantes'
Don Quixote), *The dog is turned to his
own vomit again* (from the Bible), *The
more you rub a cat on the rump, the
higher she sets her tail* (an 18th-centu-
ry proverb), and *Turn the cat in the
pan*. If reader demand is sufficient,
maybe I'll write that book.

*The phrases in this section are grouped by
animal and then alphabetized by first significant word.*

ANY MAN WHO HATES DOGS AND BABIES CAN'T BE ALL BAD

Though the record has been set straight many times over, many people still attribute this one-liner to W. C. Fields. In fact, Leo Rosten ad-libbed the remark at a testimonial dinner in 1938, on the fortieth anniversary of Fields's show-business career. Rosten later claimed that he had no idea what he was going to say, or even that he'd be called upon, but his was the showstopper to cap a long series of weepy tributes to the curmudgeonly comic actor.

Here is the full text of Rosten's speech: "The only thing I can say about W. C. Fields, whom I have admired since the day he advanced upon Baby LeRoy with an ice pick, is this: any man who hates dogs and babies can't be all bad." Several months later, after the punch line was quoted in the *Saturday Review*, it became fairly famous, though soon confusion set in as to its author. Few people still remember Rosten (author of *The Joys of Yiddish*, among other books), and as is often the case what is said by an obscure figure about a famous one sooner or later gets attributed directly to the latter. It's just the kind of phrase Fields would have been proud to coin.

TO BARK UP THE WRONG TREE

No one would accuse your average hunting dog of too
much intelligence, which is the point of this animalogy
for "looking in all the wrong places." Unbeknownst to the
hound who has treed his prey, possoms and raccoons can
jump as well as they can climb, and they're apt to be off
in some other tree by the time a pooch has barked his
alert up a tree he can't climb.

The saying originated (circa 1830) in the States, where
folks kept "coon dogs" to patrol their land. These dogs
may have been easily fooled, but people who bark up the
wrong tree are more deceived, since we usually mean that
what they're looking for was never there in the first place.

BEWARE OF THE DOG

You thought this warning dated to the time hardware
stores began selling signs? Think again, for people have
had nasty watchdogs since the classical Greeks—the
expression itself is found in Aristophanes' play *Lysistrata*
(411 B.C.). We also find the Latin version, *cave canem*,
written in Petronius's *Satyricon*, and set in mosaic among
the ruins of Pompeii. At roughly the same time as
Petronius's satire, St. Paul wrote "beware of dogs" in his
epistle to the Philippians (3:2), though I don't think he
really meant canines.

BOWWOW

The English translation of friendly barking actually seems to have a Greek ancestor, *bau bau*, found in seventh-century writings. The second *bau* or *baw* became a *waw* sometime before 1576, when William Lambarde wrote in his account of travels through Kentshire of a "Dogs barking that soundeth nothing else—but Baw waw waw." By the turn of the century this onomatopoeia had become what *The Oxford English Dictionary* calls "an exclamation of contempt," as in the anonymous play *The Distracted Emperor: A Tragi-comedy* (circa 1600): "Baw, waw, waw! Sir, trouble not your self."

The spelling, along with the usage, is now obsolete. Shakespeare tried on "bowgh wawgh" for size in *The Tempest*; Thomas Otway more or less followed suit in *Venice Preserved* (1682): "Now, bough waugh, waugh bough waugh." Anything other than "bowwow" looks strange to us, but that spelling didn't even appear until the late 18th century. We first find it, among a few contemporaneous publications, in Boswell's *Life of Samuel Johnson* (1775), where it's attributed to Lord Pembroke, who casts aspersions on Dr. Johnson's "bow-wow way," namely his tendency to snarl at dimwits.

Bowwow has since proved a very useful animalogy. Children and the childlike have been using it as a synonym for *dog* since at least the 1780s. Charles Dickens provides us with our first citation for the derivative *to go to the bow-wows,* or, as he writes, "gone to the demnition bow-wows" (*Nicholas Nickleby,* 1839). In 1892 singer Vesta Victoria had a huge hit with Joseph Tabrar's tune "Daddy Wouldn't Buy Me a Bow-Wow." Other examples of this juvenile tendency to name animals after the sounds they make—or rather, of the adult tendency to teach children to do so—are *moo-cow, tweety-bird, meow-meow, bowser,* and *woofie.*

Also notable is the phrase *bowwow theory,* a contemptuous nickname for the idea that human speech originated in the imitation of animal sounds. In 1861 Max Müller made clear, in a lecture on linguistics at the Royal Institution of Great Britain, his "strong objection" to "what I called the Bow-wow and the Pooh-pooh theories." I leave investigation of the pooh-pooh theory up to the reader.

A CYNIC

Being called a cynic is bad enough in English; it's even worse in Greek. The term traces back to a classical school of philosophy established by Antisthenes in the fourth century B.C. at a gymnasium called Cynosarges, just outside of Athens. In essence, Antisthenes preached the primacy of virtue and the worthlessness of material things. Happily enough for the school's detractors, *Cyno-*

sarges resembles *cynikos,* the Greek for "doglike"—an apt description, they thought, for a bunch not overly concerned with social custom or personal hygiene.

The most famous of the Cynics was the austere and misanthropic Diogenes, who is said to have made his home in an earthenware tub. When once asked what he thought of being called *cynikos,* Diogenes replied, "I am called a dog because I fawn on those who give me anything, I yelp at those who refuse, and I set my teeth in rascals."

This isn't generally what *cynical* means today, however. Originally, when the term began circulating in England in the 16th century, it meant "disdainful, haughty, and contemptuous of comfort." Over time it became associated with a sneering attitude toward humanity in general, and eventually, by the 19th century, it had settled into its modern meaning: "disposed to devalue people's motives." George Meredith observed in *The Egoist* (1879) that "Cynics are only happy in making the world as barren to others as they have made it for themselves"—a rather cynical assessment.

DOG DAYS

Dogs—and people—have surely suffered in the August heat since the invention of language, but in the animalogy a dog is the *cause* rather than the victim.

Indeed, the prolific Roman naturalist Pliny the Elder (first century A.D.) did claim the term has to do with the fact that "dogs are most likely to be rabid during the whole of this time"—i.e., during the hottest weeks of summer. But the Greek *hemerai kynades* ("dog days") originally referred to the so-called dog star, Sirius, which at the time rose at the beginning of August. (It now rises on August 11 at the latitude of Greenwich, England.)

According to Greek legend, Sirius was once the hunting hound of the giant Orion, who lent his own name to a proximate star. The ferocious heat coinciding with the star's ascent probably inspired the myth, as Orion's dog was said to be a pretty nasty beast.

The word *cynosure*—meaning "guiding light"—also derives from the Greek for "dog" by way of the stars. *Cynosura*, "dog's tail," was the Greek name for the constellation we call Ursa Minor, which to compound the confusion is from the Latin for "little bear." The center of that constellation is Polaris, a.k.a. the North Star, which explains our use of *cynosure*.

DOG EAT DOG

This rather disgusting animalogy was born as a negative: *Dog doesn't eat dog.* This sensible observation was actually a play on words rather than a scientific hypothesis. Coined around the first century B.C., *Canis caninam non est*—"dogs are not dog-eaters"—puns on the earlier saying, itself a pun, *Canis a non canendo*—"the name *dog* (*canis*) comes from the fact that they can't sing (*non canendo*)."

And that's a lot of work for a simple proverb meaning "people leave their own kind alone." Various other creatures were employed to make the same point; "Wild beasts do not injure beasts spotted like themselves," quoth Juvenal (second century A.D.). Shakespeare was the English pioneer, writing in *Much Ado about Nothing* (1598) that "Two bears will not bite one another when they meet," and in *Troilus and Cressida* (1601) that "One bear will not bite another." A version involving wolves was current later in the 17th century.

The exception to the rule was first propounded in 1732 by Thomas Fuller in a collection of pearls of wisdom. "Dogs are hard drove, when they eat dogs," he observes, later adding that "It is an hard Winter, when Dogs eat Dogs." Whether Fuller ever observed such a thing is questionable; nevertheless his philosophy, dormant for a couple of centuries, made a big comeback in the 20th century, as the expression *it's a dog-eat-dog world* became popular. Which says a lot more about modern life than it does about dogs. As C. H. Spurgeon wrote in 1869, "Dog won't eat dog, but men will eat each other up like cannibals."

EVERY DOG HAS ITS DAY

The first dog to have his day claimed it at the expense of
the Greek playwright Euripides, in a real rather than fic-
tional tragedy.

These were the days when drama was taken very seriously indeed and when dramatic contests were a highlight of your average Greek games. In 406 B.C. Euripides
was vacationing in Macedonia after one of his triumphs.
One sore loser happened to catch wind of Euripides' visit
and rounded up a pack of dogs, which obediently tore
Euripides to pieces.

Leave it to the Greeks to make a proverb out of car-
nage; in the historian Plutarch's version (circa A.D. 95), it
goes, "Even a dog gets his revenge." (Never mind that the
canines in question had nothing personal against their
victim; hate me, hate my dog.) This saying, passed down
through the usual channels (collections of moralistic ad-
ages), was translated into English by Richard Taverner
in 1539: "A dogge hath a day." As Taverner explains it,
"There is none so vyle or symple a person but at one tyme
or other may avenge him selfe of wronges done unto hym."

Taverner's version was a big hit in England, being
quoted by no less a personage than Queen Elizabeth I,
who early in her career said, "As a dog hath a day, so may
I perchance have time to declare it in deeds." (Offhand,
I'm not sure what she was referring to, but it could have

been anything, since you didn't have to look hard to find doubters and naysayers at that point.) The more familiar *Every dog has his day* would appear only over a century later.

TO GO TO THE DOGS

Things have been "going to the dogs" for hundreds of years—even thousands, if you count Greek dramatist Aristophanes' line "to go to the crows," found in numerous plays (fifth century B.C.). Crows, canines, it's all the same: you don't want to go there.

A dog's life has never been all that pretty, and the species has been an object of contempt, not love, in many cultures. The comparison wasn't flattering, for instance, in Renaissance England, where this phrase was coined. People have been carping ever since about the way things are going to the dogs; it's a tune that never changes, a point wittily noted in this anonymous poem of the early 20th century:

> My grandad, viewing the earth's worn cogs,
> Said, "Things are going to the dogs";
> His grandad in his house of logs
> Swore things were going to the dogs;
> His grandad in the Flemish bogs
> Swore things were going to the dogs;
> His grandad in his old skin togs

Said, "Things are going to the dogs."
Well, there's one thing I have to state:
Those dogs have had a good long wait.

HAIR OF THE DOG

Back in ancient Rome, this phrase was more than a figure of speech—it was a medical prescription. The
Romans were heavily into alternative medicine and
homeopathy—"like cures like" was their medical watch-
word. So if you saw a Roman walking around with a patch
of dog hair stuck to his skin, you knew it was the hair of
the dog that bit him, for that was thought the best medicine. (I know, hair isn't "like" a dog bite; the remedy just
had to come from the same source as the illness.)

Believe it or not, this piece of folk medicine persisted
for centuries, almost into the 18th century, though by the
medieval period the prescription had become *burnt* hair
of the dog that bit you. Raw or cooked, though, the hair
probably had little effect on the bite, except maybe to act
as a crude Band-Aid. Similarly cosmetic is the modern
version of hair of the dog, namely a stiff one in the morning to "cure" a hangover. (Dull the pain is more like it.)

The belief that liquor is quicker the morning after is
pretty old, though not as old as the hair-of-the-dog cure
from which it takes its name. By the mid-16th century
the notion was already proverbial; in 1546 John Heywood

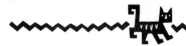

cited the line "I pray thee let me and my fellow have a hair of the dog that bit us last night—and bitten were we both to the brain aright."

A HANGDOG LOOK

Have you ever stopped to think about this one? The obvious conclusion is that it has something to do with that special expression of the miserable pooch and the prominent "hanging" of the corners of their frowns. Imagine my surprise when I turned up many old sayings and stories of literal dog hanging.

Dogs and other animals convicted in courts of committing serious "crimes" were sent to the gallows just like human malefactors. This was before there was any real concept of criminal "intention"; acts were judged on their face, and you were punished for the evil you did whether or not you "meant" it. So a dog could be just as criminal as a man.

William and Mary Morris indirectly quote as an authority *The Coasts of Illusion* (1924) by Clark B. Firestone, who reported that "Domestic animals which had killed or maimed persons were regularly tried in the criminal courts of Greece and medieval Europe. Ecclesiastical courts long exercised jurisdiction over smaller animal offenders … there is a record of 144 successful prosecutions of animals, vermin included." There are even a few specific reports of dogs being hanged in England—the earliest being in 1595 (for "inflicting a fatal injury on a child's finger").

As for *hangdog look*, it's hard to tell whether it refers to the expression of someone who hangs dogs, or to the look on the face of the doomed dog itself. If we're to trust *The Oxford English Dictionary,* originally *hang-dog* was the word for a "dispicable or degraded fellow fit only to hang a dog, or be hanged like a dog." From there it came to mean "low, degraded; having a base or sneaking appearance."

HIS BARK IS WORSE THAN HIS BITE

It's ancient wisdom that yappy dogs are safer than the silent type. "Cowardly dogs bite the less the worse they bark," quoth Quintus Curtius Rufus, a forgotten Roman historian of the first century. An English adaptation appears in the 14th century: "It is the manner of the fee-blest hounds for to bark most." In other words, cowards and weaklings make the biggest threats.

There's an equivalent expression in practically every language. *Il fait plus de bruit que de mal,* say the French—"He causes more noise than injury." The old Italian saying is *Cane che baia, non suol nocer,* translated by John Florio (1578) as "A barking dog hurteth not." A common English proverb of the 16th through 18th centuries was "Great barkers are no biters"; its complement is "The slowest barker is the surest biter," which is found as early as 1270 and as late as Arthur Conan Doyle's *Sir Nigel* (1906). The latter ultimately traces to the Latin proverb, *Cave tibi a cane muto et aqua silenti*: "Beware of a silent dog and still water."

HOT DOG

Why is a frankfurter called a *hot dog*? Apparently the term was coined around the turn of the century by sports cartoonist T. A. Dorgan, who'd heard a rumor that the franks were made from dog-meat. His subsequent caricature of a dachshund on a bun got the goat of the Coney Island Chamber of Commerce, where the delicacy was seeing most of its business. (Actually, Dorgan had bought his frank at the New York Polo Grounds, the Giants'

home park, where the sandwich was first sold.)

Whether or not this story is true, Dorgan wouldn't have been the first to put the two words *hot* and *dog* together. While only stray citations are found before 1900, by that date it already had several applications. Here's the definition from an issue that year of *Dialect Notes*: "*Hot-dog*. 1. One very proficient in certain things. 2. A hot sausage. 3. A hard student. 4. A conceited person." I've never heard *hot dog* used the third way, but the other definitions survive. *Hot dog!* the exclamation made its debut a few years later, but *hot diggity dog!* would have to wait a couple decades.

LET SLEEPING DOGS LIE

If there's anything more unpleasant than I am before my morning caffeine, it's a dog aroused from its nap—or so folk wisdom would have it. Actually, the basic idea goes back at least to Sophocles' *Oedipus Rex* (circa 409 B.C.), where we find the line "'Twere better to leave sleeping ills at rest."

But why substitute *dogs* for *ills*? After all, any number of animals (such as rattlesnakes) are more dangerous when roused. And, oddly enough, a *less* dangerous animal—the housecat—is found in the current French version of the phrase. I'm sure we'll never know why dogs got picked on; what we do know is that it was again the

French who probably did it first, for our earliest citation is this 13th-century proverb: *Il fait mal éveiller le chien qui dort* ("It's a bad idea to wake a sleeping dog").

Dogs have been the regular targets in English since Chaucer's day; in *Troilus and Criseyde* (circa 1380), he writes, without explaining, "It is nought good a sleeping hound to wake." The modern version probably traces to the later 18th century, and is first found in writing in the earlier 19th. The novelist Sir Walter Scott advises, in *Redgauntlet* (1824), that it is "best to let sleeping dogs lie"; Charles Dickens trimmed off the "best to" in *David Copperfield* (1850).

LOVE ME, LOVE MY DOG

Though later a command—practically a threat—this phrase was originally just descriptive. It was coined by Saint Bernard of Clairvaux, who proclaimed in a 12th-century sermon that *Qui me amat, amat et canem meum* ("Who loves me, loves my dog"). Bernard seems to have meant that the hound is an extension of the man—his vigilant protector, his companion, and his guide. You simply could not love someone, therefore, without loving the pooch. (Notice that nobody says, "Love me, love my spouse.")

All the early English citations are, like Bernard's, just statements of fact. But by the later 17th century, every-

one understood it as a command. "Love me, love my dog," wrote Sir Roger L'Estrange in his very popular *Fables* (1692), "for there are certain decencies of respect due the servant for the master's sake."

The really strange news, though, is that the Saint Bernard in question isn't the dog's namesake—that's another Saint Bernard, of Menthon, who lived about a century before the other. This older Bernard built a hospice on an Alpine pass subsequently dubbed the "Great St. Bernard Pass." The canons who ran this hospice bred the dogs to rescue travelers lost in the snow, and presumably named them, too.

MAN BITES DOG

Most often used as a nickname for cute, "can-you-beat-that"–type media stories, this phrase was coined by John Bogart, an editor at the *New York Sun* in the late 19th century. "When a dog bites a man," said Bogart, "that is not news, because it happens so often. But if a man bites a dog, that is news." A more precise description of the tabloid ethic cannot be imagined.

TO PUT ON DOG

We may pretty precisely trace this saying to fun-loving Yale University in the 1860s, for it is defined for the general public by a former student. "*To put on dog*," writes Lyman H. Bagg in *Four Years at Yale* (circa 1869), "is to make a flashy display, to cut a swell." In case there were any doubt about it, A. H. Lewis clears that up with this apposition from his *Wolfville* (1897): "The Dallas sharp, puttin' on a heap of hawtoor an' dog." For "hawtoor" read *hauteur*, a term almost as fancy as *dog*.

What the Yale wits meant is anyone's guess. It's likely, however, that the metaphor was always supposed to be a little ridiculous. Both *The Oxford English Dictionary* and *Brewer's Dictionary* define the phrase as a rebuke of putting on airs, with the *OED* citing may early examples, including Lewis's. It may be possible to employ *put on dog* (later *the dog*) without sarcasm, but it's hard to imagine anyone's welcoming the canine comparison.

If the phrase was ironic from the start, it probably referred to dogs' somewhat foolish attempts to act dignified. As satirist Samuel Butler wrote in his *Note-Books* (circa 1890), "The great pleasure of a dog is that you may make a fool of yourself with him and not only will he not scold you, but he will make a fool of himself too."

A SHAGGY-DOG STORY

The original shaggy-dog stories actually *were* stories about shaggy dogs. In fact, such tales were a major fad in the '40s, especially after the end of the war. Their subject was sometimes a talking dog, sometimes the companion of a wandering knight, sometimes an entrant in a shaggy-dog contest, sometimes just a dog passing through.

What all these tales had in common besides hirsute hounds is that they were long, pointless, and absurd. Even when the dog disappeared from the genre, shaggy-dog stories remained digressive and anticlimactic, often ending (though not concluding) with a bad pun. Excellent examples are still heard every week on the BBC radio program *My Word!*

AN UNDERDOG

To those of us of a certain age, Underdog was a caped cartoon character. But the word goes way back to the 19th century, when cartoons were but a gleam in Walt Disney's father's eye and American songwriter David Barker penned "The Under Dog in a Fight" (first published 1876). Here are a few inspiring verses:

> [F]or me,—and I care not a single fig
>   If they say I am wrong or am right,—
> I shall always go for the weaker dog,
>   For the under dog in the fight.
> I know that the world, that the great big world,
>
>   Will never a moment stop
> To see which dog may be in the fault,
>   But will shout for the dog on top.

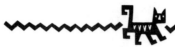

But for me, I shall never pause to ask
    Which dog may be in the right,
For my heart will beat, while it beats at all,
    For the under dog in the fight.

As Barker admits, he doesn't give more of a fig about right or wrong than those who cheer on the "top dog." He is simply of the breed that feels for the "under dog," no matter which dog picked the fight.

It may be a silly reason to burst into song, but the tune did leave its mark on our language. By the 1890s Barker's coinage was being used to describe the losing party of a political contest, and by the 1930s the word *underdoggery* had been forged to describe sentiments like his.

TO RAIN CATS AND DOGS

This phrase, so often heard, is poorly understood, though lexicographers will always take an imaginative crack at it. The only thing we do know is that the first printed reference (1652) is actually to "dogs and polecats" (relatives of skunks).

Robert Hendrickson, among those who theorize, suggests that perhaps *to rain cats and dogs* refers to terrible 17th-century storms when dead dogs and cats would wash down the gutterless streets. He admits to being stymied by the polecats, though, and that the phrase as we know it wasn't printed until the late 18th century, in a work by Swift. Then perhaps, he continues, the saying derives from the obscure French term *catadoupe*, "waterfall."

William and Mary Morris prefer a more mythic origin, pointing out that sailors in the Dark Ages believed that witches cause storms and then ride on them in the form of black cats. Dogs, meanwhile, were the ancient companions of Odin, storm god of Norse mythology. Thus, cats = rain, and dogs = wind. Couldn't be more obvious.

TO BELL THE CAT

Here's another phrase we owe to Aesop. According to the fable of "The Mice in Council," all the rodents of a house got together to debate how to deal with a stealthy new cat, who'd been dining very well at their expense.

One clever mouse rose to put forth this plan: "What we should do," he said, "is fasten a bell around the neck of our enemy the cat; its tinkling will then warn us of her approach." This plan was warmly applauded until an even wiser old mouse got up and said, "Who, may I ask, is going to bell the cat?" Though the fable ends there, we gather there were no volunteers.

To bell the cat, therefore, is to put yourself at great risk for the common good. History offers few examples, but there is the case of a Scotsman, Archibald, Earl of Angus. This was during the reign of James III (mid-15th century), when to the consternation of the old nobility the king elevated mere artists to the peerage. Various nobles gathered to grumble and plot the demise of the new Earl of Mar, Robert Cochrane, an architect and a particular favorite of James's. The Lord Grey asked rhetorically, "Who will bell the cat?" Archibald quickly volunteered and, true to his word, had Cochrane captured and hanged. Forever after, the Earl of Angus was known as "Bell-the-Cat."

Aesop tells several other amusing tales of wars between cats and mice. Another good one is "The Cat and the Mice," wherein the housecat seeks to coax mouse-snacks out of their holes by hanging herself down by the hind legs from a peg and playing possum. The mice are too smart to buy this charade. From its safe spot in the wall, one calls out, "Very clever, madam; but you may turn yourself into a sack of meal hanging there if you like, but you still won't catch any of us coming near you."

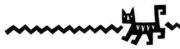

A CAT'S NINE LIVES

Cats *do* seem naturally blessed with a special agility and tenacity. But if they have "nine lives," each is a couple of years long at best. (Rare is the cat who lives to see 20).

Where this superstition originated is impossible to know, though perhaps it traces to ancient Egypt, where it was thought cats had all kinds of special powers. (The Egyptians were presumably first to domesticate cats.) At the very latest the notion dates to the eighth century B.C., for we find it in a collection of Indian fables written about then. English versions, which date to the 16th century, seem already to presume this astonishing fact, for the common form is "A woman has nine lives like a cat"— the new information here has to do with women, not cats. Thomas Fuller took this analogy further in *Gnomologia* (1732): "A Cat has nine Lives, and a Woman has nine Cat Lives," that is, 81 opportunities to make a fatal mistake.

• **See also:** *not enough room to swing a cat* (page 103).

A CAT'S-PAW

Someone's "cat's-paw" is his dupe—the guy or gal saddled with the dirty work. This strange idiom derives from the even stranger 17th-century emblem of a monkey using a cat's paw to pull chestnuts out of a fire.

Why? Because the monkey craved the chestnuts, but

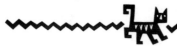

didn't care to take the heat. Apparently the original tale, which was Arabic, featured a monkey using a dog's paw to pull a crab from the fire. And early European versions also have *dog* for *cat*, though nuts had already been substituted for the crab.

As for how cats figure in the story, somebody may have misunderstood the Latin word *catellus*, "puppy." An easy mistake; less explicable is why some Italian, Spanish, and Dutch versions give *snake* instead of either *nuts* or *crabs*. No matter; by the 18th century *cat's-paw* was the regular saying in English, with *nuts* left understood.

KITTY-CORNER

Kitty-corner, sometimes written *catty-corner* or *cater-corner*, has nothing to do with cats crossing an intersection. It's from the French *quatre* (pronounced KAT-tr'), "four." *Cater* is the best English speakers could do with that one,

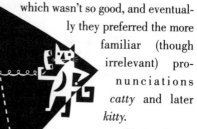

which wasn't so good, and eventually they preferred the more familiar (though irrelevant) pronunciations *catty* and later *kitty*.

Obviously, a four-cornered (*quatre-*

cornered) intersection has four corners, not all of which are diagonally opposed. Thus our particular use of the phrase is difficult to justify. Perhaps the reasoning is that for two corners to be kitty, you've got to have four in all.

Though this *cater* isn't feline, the *cater-* of *caterpillar* is. It comes from the Old North French *catepelose,* "hairy cat," which is really kind of a stretch, conceptually.

TO LET THE CAT OUT OF THE BAG

There are a couple of likely stories about this phrase. For example: that *cat* really means "cat-o'-nine-tails," just as in *not enough room to swing a cat* (see page 103). This sort of cat was a common instrument of punishment aboard British naval vessels; it was thus a ship's master-at-arms who "let the cat out of the bag" (its red carrying case) prior to a flogging.

The problem with this explanation for a phrase meaning "to give away a secret" is that it makes no sense. A little better is the theory that the phrase goes back to English country fairs of olden times. A popular scam was to advertise "pigs in pokes," that is, suckling porkers packaged in sacks. (*Poke,* meaning "bag," shares an origin with *pocket.*) Unfortunately for the suckers who bought one, what they were getting wasn't a pig but an old cat. Wiser heads would sometimes spare the victim by opening the sack before it was sold, thus "letting the cat

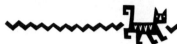

out of the bag." They say this trick was practiced at fairs for centuries, but I have a hard time believing people could be that stupid for that long.

Obviously, this latter scenario (or something like it) is also the origin of the saying *to buy a pig in a poke,* meaning "to buy blind." It was once a little ethical proverb in 16th-century England that "When ye proffer the pig, open the poke." This predates *to let the cat out of the bag* by a couple of hundred years.

LIKE A CAT ON A HOT TIN ROOF

Apparently cats have been spied—or imagined—dancing on hot surfaces since long before the days of tin roofs. In a 17th-century English proverb book, for example, we find *like a cat upon hot bake-stone* (meaning "hot bricks," which was in fact later substituted).

As you can well imagine if you've ever walked pavement barefoot on a dog day, cats lose their typical nonchalance on hot bake-stone or hot anything. In fact, they get a little frantic, which accounts for the full original phrasing, *nervous as a cat on a hot tin roof.* Only the short form is well known today, thanks mostly to Tennessee Williams.

NOT ROOM ENOUGH TO SWING A CAT

Perhaps you feel as Mr. Dick did in Charles Dickens's *David Copperfield* (1849): "You know, Trotwood, I don't want to swing a cat. I never do swing a cat. Therefore what does that signify to *me*!"

Personally, I *have* met a few cats I'd like to swing, but the phrase actually has nothing to do with housepets. This "cat" is a cat-o'-nine-tails—that is, a whip. *Cat* just happened to be a familiar abbreviation when the phrase was coined, in the late 18th century. Now, that's a cat I really don't want to swing.

In case you're wondering, a cat-o'-nine-tails is a whip made of nine knotted lashes, originally devised principally for use against miscreants in the British army and navy. The precise origin of the term, first recorded in the later 17th century, is unknown, though *The Oxford English Dictionary* guesses it's a grimly humorous reference to the way the instrument "scratches" the back. It may also have something to do with the number nine, which

as we know from their reputed "nine lives" (see page 99) has always had some sort of mystical association with the feline species.

SITTING IN THE CATBIRD SEAT

There's a long story behind the phrase *to sit in the catbird seat,* meaning "to sit pretty," but it doesn't amount to an explanation. James Thurber brought it to the literary set with his story "The Catbird Seat" (1942), but he admitted to borrowing it from baseball sportscaster Red Barber, who covered the Brooklyn Dodgers in those days. Barber, a southerner, peppered his commentary with all sorts of catchy coinages, some of which were his own. But he got *sitting in the catbird seat* from a poker partner, who'd used it to describe holding a surefire winning hand. This fellow probably pulled it from the air; scholars think the phrase was spoken as early as the 19th century.

So, what does it actually mean? *Catbird* is easily explained: it's another name for a thrush, whose call sounds sort of like "meow." *Seat* probably refers to the fact that thrushes like to perch high in trees, beyond the reach of earthbound creatures. Of course, lots of birds perch high in trees, but *catbird seat* does have a certain ring.

THERE'S MORE THAN ONE WAY TO SKIN A CAT

No doubt. But isn't one more than sufficient?

Slightly more sensible is the original version, found in Charles Kingsley's romance *Westward Ho!* (1855): "There are more ways of killing a cat than choking her

with cream." (I said "slightly.") That this method is rather unlikely to work is more or less the point. The gist is that if one of your ideas has failed or is likely to fail, don't give up, for there's probably a more elegant and effective way of doing the job.

Actually, Kingsley can't really be credited with inventing this phrase whole, for in a 1678 collection of English proverbs we find, "There are more ways to kill a dog than hanging." More recent authors have indeed ignored the doggie version and played some interesting variations on Kingsley's. "There is more than one way to kill a cat," wrote H. W. Thompson in 1940, "besides soaking him in butter." Two years later Mary Lasswell presented this compromise in *Suds in Your Eye*: "There's more ways o' killin' a cat than chokin' it to death with butter." Best of all, however, is Matthew Head's technique in *The Smell of Money* (1943): "There's more ways to kill a cat than throwing the grand piano at it."

The simpler version—sans cream, butter, or grand pianos—first shows up in Mark Twain's *Connecticut Yankee in King Arthur's Court* (1889): "She knew more than one way to skin a cat."

WHEN THE CAT'S AWAY, THE MICE WILL PLAY

Elizabethan translator John Florio almost got it right when he rendered an old Italian saying as "When the Cat is abroad, the Mice play." Except that the original, *Quando la gatta non è in casa, i sorsi ballano,* really means, "When the cat's not at home, the mice dance." If Florio was going to get it wrong, he might at least have rhymed.

Many have been the variations on this interesting theme. Thomas Heywood snagged the rhyme, giving us the familiar version, in his play *A Woman Kilde with Kindness* (1607): "There's an old proverb—when the cat's away, the mouse may play." But that didn't stop physician Thomas Fuller from trying to palm off his own version in 1670: "When the cat's gone, the mice grow saucy." Going back a ways, we find another angle in the *Adagia* of Desiderius Erasmus (1508), a compendium of Latin proverbs: "There be no goodness of sheep, if the shepherd be away." Even more ancient is this line from *Persa,* a comedy by the Roman dramatist Plautus (circa 200 B.C.): "Sport as you may while the master's away."

Romans and Englishmen aren't the only ones to make such incisive observations of human behavior. The French say something like, "When the cat runs over the roofs, the mice dance across the floors." According to the Chinese, who apparently said it first, "When the cat's away, the rats come out to stretch." Most penetrating of all is the Japanese proverb, "When the devil is away, let us wash our clothes."

Silly Geese

This chapter is for just plain strange animalogies, which only seem stranger if you think about them ("Charley horse"?). In fact, while some are legitimately odd, others make perfect sense once you know the story behind them ("There once was a horse named Charley…").

Also included here are a few odds and ends that didn't fit the other chapters, most of them describing animal abuse—taking bulls by the horns, beating dead horses, and so on. Since these aren't generally things you'd ever want to do, "silly" is as good a description as any.

The phrases in this section are alphabetized by their first significant word.

ADAM'S OFF OX

This odd American expression came back into vogue in the early 1990s, when the press briefly fixated on its use by then-candidate Bill Clinton. It's natural to assume the saying's one of those colorful barnyard southernisms, but in fact it was first recorded in an 1848 book, *Nantucketisms,* on the idioms of the Massachusetts island.

The original version was *poor as God's off ox,* while the recent style is *I don't know him from Adam's off ox,* an obvious derivative of *I wouldn't know him from Adam.* But what's an "off ox," and why should it be poor *or* obscure?

The off ox of a yoke of oxen is the rightmost, and thus the farthest from the driver, who rides to the left. Being last in line, as it were, the off ox would get the least attention, and so easily lend itself to a metaphor for "ill-rewarded" or "least known." Occasionally *off ox* appears on its own and means "klutz," since real off oxen are the most apt of the team to stumble and fall.

TO BEARD THE LION IN ITS DEN

Today this phrase is a metaphor for uncommon bravery (or foolhardiness). What it literally means is "to enter a lion's own den and pull its beard" (not cut it off), which is akin, say, to walking into the boss's office and telling

him off. The trick is to get away with it.

Getting away with it easily, rather than the courage in doing it, was in fact the entire point of the original saying. *Hares may pull dead lions by the beard,* found in several texts of the later 16th century, is rather more scornful than its familiar descendent. A hare is the animalogical epitome of cowardice, as the lion is of courage; and pulling somebody's beard used to be a very grave insult. So the point of the old saying is pretty clear, and it's not a compliment. Cowards may easily indulge in false bravado.

The Renaissance saying seemingly goes back to an old Latin saying, *Hares will leap at dead lions.* The English contribution was the beard. Also British is *bearding the lion in its den,* a line first found in Sir Walter Scott's poem *Marmion* (1808).

BEATING A DEAD HORSE

Also known as *flogging a dead horse,* this practice was first noted in a comedy by the Roman playwright Plautus circa 200 B.C. But dead horses have a tradition all their own in the English language, which goes back to the 17th-century saying *to work for a dead horse,* meaning to work for nothing, or rather to work for pay you've already spent. (*Dead horse* on its own could mean "spent wages" or "an exhausted paycheck"; apparently the slang was

popular among British sailors for advance pay, which was already spent long before they'd earned it.)

Phrases such as *working a dead horse, playing a dead horse, mounting a dead horse,* etc.—all more or less referring to fruitless labor—precede the more familiar *flogging a dead horse* in English by a couple hundred years. The coinage is usually credited to British states-man John Bright, who used it in 1867 to characterize efforts to knock some sense into Parliament. Bright didn't say whether he had Plautus in mind.

As to *flog* versus *beat,* while the latter's more common now, the original is more precise, since *flog* is exactly the word for what you do to put some spirit into a horse. Flogging a dead horse is thus obviously futile, but even more it implies the flogger is so out of it or so bent on his purpose that he doesn't even notice the horse has expired.

A CHARLEY HORSE

The most common account for this expression is that it traces back to an unlucky steed named Charley who bit the dust after getting a very nasty "Charley horse." Some say that Charley worked for the Chicago White Sox in the 1890s and suffered his fate while pulling a roller over the infield.

But the phrase is older than that, though still apropos

baseball. In *Play Ball* (1888), M. J. Kelley wrote that he "never was bothered with 'Charley Horse'"; and a year later, a Cincinnati columnist wrote of the sad story of "Mac," who "was affected with a 'Charley-horse' and that ended his ball-playing for 1888." The mysterious phrase has ever since been most often applied to the overpaid boys of summer.

TO COOK ONE'S GOOSE

According to old English chronicles, which aren't terribly reliable, this saying goes back to the 16th century and King Erik XIV of Sweden. As the story goes, the king (who would later become mentally deranged) advanced with a handful of men upon an enemy town, whose residents were unimpressed by the tiny band. The townsmen mockingly hung up a goose (legendary for stupidity) from a tower, but the laugh was on them. By nightfall Erik and his men had breached the town walls and begun to burn the place down. "What do you mean by this?" cried the townsmen. "To cook your goose!" retorted the king.

Perhaps. Anyway, the phrase just sat in the chronicles until the mid-19th century, when it was coined anew by someone who probably never heard of "Mad Erik." In 1851 anonymous parties published a broadside ballad attacking Pope Pius IX, who was looking to win more English converts. The staunchly Protestant authors

promised to "cook" his "goose," along with that of the new English cardinal. Once again, they probably chose *goose* because it was more or less synonymous with *idiot*.

A DINGBAT

This versatile term for typographic ornaments and dolts refers to an animal that exists only in literature. Some lexicographers suggest that the term derives from *batty* or *bats* plus the Dutch *ding*, "thing." Less lame is the theory that the origin is *the dingbats*, Australian slang for delirium tremens—but that raises chicken/egg problems. Or maybe the phrase is related to *ding-dang*, as in *ding-dang fool*, an Americanism from around the turn of the century.

The best theory of all, though, is based on the fact that when *dingbat* first surfaced, around 1860 in America, it meant "a small object easily thrown at another." The probable origin is a union of *bat* (as in "stick of wood") with *ding* (old slang for "throw," from a verb that originally meant "beat" or "flog").

If this is true, then *dingbat* soon came to mean simply "small object," thrown or not, which explains its use in the printing trade. From there it was used as a proxy word, akin to *doohickey*, for "that thing I don't know the name of." How it got to mean "crazy" or "stupid" is unknown, but it may have to do with the funny sound of the word itself.

AN ELEPHANT NEVER FORGETS

Lack of familiarity breeds some strange ideas. If medieval bestiaries are at all indicative of their time, westerners were once willing to believe that elephants "have no desire to copulate" and that they "live three hundred years" (*The Book of Beasts*). Perhaps the latter myth is the source of our notions about elephants' prodigious memories—age being traditionally associated with wisdom and retrospection.

As it happens, elephants don't live even as long as human beings. And the only data on their memories is purely anecdotal. A typical story cites an elephant in the

Bronx Zoo who took a strange disliking to one of his attendants. One day, after several years' absence, the man returned; the elephant recognized him in an instant and attempted to break out of his cage to do his nemesis some mischief.

Stories like this are about the best we can do; in other words, elephants may be more retentive than other species, but probably not by much. Another legend for the myth file is that elephants are terrified of mice, supposedly because they fear the little critters will get up in their trunks. Equally false is the belief that elephants drink through their trunks; they do suck up water that way, but then squirt it into their mouths. On the other hand, elephants do love peanuts.

TO GO WHOLE HOG

This expression for stopping at nothing is usually said to trace to an old Muslim tale. An English version may be found, among other places, in William Cowper's poem "The Love of the World" (1779).

It seems that Mohammed instructed his followers that they might eat every part of a pig save one, which he didn't name. For fear of violating this law most believers refrained from pork altogether; but a certain pragmatic bunch of imams "thought it hard," as Cowper writes, "From the whole hog to be debarred." "He couldn't have meant the leg," thought the first, pulling that part off a freshly-roasted pig; "But of course Mohammed permitted the shoulder," thought the second, helping himself to that piece. One by one each picked at the roast, till the "whole hog" was gone.

If we accept this as its origin, the phrase originally referred to throwing caution to the winds, or more plainly

to a shameful lack of restraint. But many doubt this origin. More likely the phrase plays on the 17th-century English slang *hog*, meaning "shilling"; "to go whole hog" was to spend the entire sum on one piece of pleasure. This was back when a shilling was actually worth something.

Americans shouldn't feel too left out; *hog* was slang here for a dime. And besides, the phrase in the form *to go the whole hog* originated here in the 1820s. (It was first applied to President Andrew Jackson.)

GROUNDHOG DAY

Everyone looks forward to February 2, when the news is enlivened by many fascinating stories of the groundhog and its shadow. Tradition has it that the groundhog, a.k.a. the woodchuck, emerges on that day from its hibernation to take stock of the weather. If the sun casts a shadow, the hog deduces six more weeks of unpleasantness and goes back to sleep. If on the other hand it's cloudy, that means the rest of winter will be mild and that it's safe to come out and start chucking wood.

Of course, anybody is capable of observing whether the day is sunny or cloudy and then of making dubious generalizations from the data. (Neither a groundhog nor a weatherman can tell you much from one day's weather.) Nonetheless, reporters swoop down upon the town of Punxsutawney, Pennsylvania, to record the rituals of

"Punxsutawney Phil," the most famous groundhog in America and its chief meteorological arbiter. Sometimes Phil (a name passed down through groundhog generations) has to be roused from his slumber, since hibernation doesn't end precisely on February 2 every year.

It's difficult to say where this tradition originated, but according to the best available theory it was imported to the U.S. by the Pilgrims, who had used hedgehogs for the very purpose in England. (Germans preferred badgers.) Since hedgehogs are considerably rarer Stateside, the settlers went for the next best thing.

HOGWASH

In the olden days of the 15th century, *hogwash* was neither an exclamation nor a metaphor. It was the name for literal slop, in other words, kitchen garbage—stuff fit only for hogs.

But why was *hogwash* slop and not porcine bathwater? Because in the 15th century *wash* meant first "wastewater" and later simply "waste"; by the 16th century it came to be specially associated with pigs. In his grim little volume *Pilgrimage to Paradise* (1592), Nicholas Breton wrote, "The sweetest wine is but as swinish wash,/ Unto the water of the well of life." More vividly, the future King Henry IV poetically notes, in Shakespeare's *Richard III,* that "The wretched, bloody, and usurping

boar, ... / Swills your warm blood like wash, and makes his trough/ In your embowelled bosoms." He means King Richard, better known for his want of a horse than for his affiliation with swine.

HUSH PUPPIES

These, um, delicious treats of fried cornmeal batter are a popular side-dish in the South. Where the name came from is another story; all the explanations are pretty unlikely. One story is that southern cooks, whose frying fish attracted packs of barking dogs, would toss them corn fritters and cry, "Hush, puppies!" A variation traces the name to the Reconstruction era, when food was scarce and cornmeal a staple; bawling children and howling dogs would be served a few morsels and be told to hush. (Actually, though, the term doesn't appear in print until the 1910s.)

There are many other stories, but they're way out there. As for the comfy loafers called Hush Puppies, these were trademarked in 1961 by the Wolverine Shoe and Tanning Company, perhaps by some association of the food with shoe leather.

A KANGAROO COURT

According to William S. Walsh in his compendious *Handy-Book*, the kangaroo got its name when Captain James Cook "discovered" Australia in 1770. From his boat Cook spied natives gathered on the shore with a curious-looking (but dead) beast and sent some of his men ashore to investigate. Attempting in vain to make themselves understood, the sailors received from the natives only a shrug and the reply "I don't know [what you're talking about]"—*kan ga roo* in the aboriginal tongue. Misunderstanding all round thus produced the animal's English name. (Cook spelled it "Kangooroo" in his journal.)

Unfortunately, logic decides against this tale. After all, even if *kan ga roo* meant "I don't know," nobody could have known that at the time. And after settling, Englishmen would have to have discovered sooner or later that the natives had a different word for the creature. In fact, the most likely explanation is that *kan ga roo* was the animal's name in an aboriginal dialect, and that the familiar story is just a tall tale.

Kangaroo court is another Americanism, with origins in the mid-19th century. Appearing in print by 1853, the phrase originally referred, according to A. J. Pollock, to "a jail tribunal comprised of inmates which collects money from prisoners awaiting trial to supply the needy

with tobacco, food and a few luxuries—its decision regarding disputes is final" (*The Underworld Speaks*, 1935). This peculiar definition gave way to the more general and now more familiar one—"a trial of sham justice, in which a guilty verdict is predetermined"—only in the 1960s, when we first find *kangaroo court* used this way in the *Times* of London.

But why *kangaroo court* for "sham trial"? The name may trace back to the days when Australia was Britain's chief penal colony: most of the English inhabitants were prisoners. It may have been there that such mock prison trials were instituted to deal with those who transgressed the code. Or perhaps the term alludes to the blank stares of kangaroos gathered beyond range of human spears, stares that recalled those of jurors at a mock trial. Whether these or any of the other fanciful etymologies are correct, the term was first recorded in America during the California gold rush.

A LOUNGE LIZARD

The *lizard* part's easy—these reptiles, like their human counterparts, are cold-blooded and quick to pounce. It's the *lounge* part that's hard. We can't be sure whether it originally stemmed from the verb—describing the sleazy operator's technique of lounging about in ladies' parlors waiting for the opportunity to strike—or from the noun—

describing the sort of place he could be found stalking his prey. In either case, *lounge lizard* flourished in the '20s and survives today as a mock at nightclub sleazoids.

MOTH-EATEN

It's fine to use this phrase for ratty old clothes (or ratty old ideas), so long as you know it's really a mistake. Moths don't have the equipment to "eat" anything; their mouths are just soft tubes, and they couldn't damage paper, let alone sturdy woolens. It's *caterpillars* that wreak havoc in your closet, though I suppose you can blame mama moths for that, since they like to lay their eggs in warm, woolly places.

PIG LATIN

Igpay Atlinlay isway eallyray unfay! But it used to be even more fun, when pig Latin was a doggerel of Latin and English—which is why it was originally called *dog Latin.* The *pig* part was somebody's idea of improving the phrase, since it sounds (slightly) more like oinking than barking.

Dog Latin and dog Greek go back to the 1700s; we don't have a precise date for the invention of the pig Latin spoken by children and jokesters today, though it goes back at least to World War I. (The first printed men-

tion is in a 1937 Raymond Chandler story.) Since then, a handful of pig-Latin perversions have taken on a life of their own in slang: *ixnay* and *amscray*, for example. It's also possible that *ofay*— old African-American dialect, dating to the '20s, for members of the opposite race— comes from the pig Latin for *foe*, though I wouldn't bet on it.

TO RIDE A HIGH HORSE

In the olden days, people of high rank really did ride high horses in pageants and processions. The biggest and best horses were reserved for such displays, and for the occasional important battle. Needless to say, the crowd had ambivalent feelings about the kings, queens, lords, and ladies whose honor befitted the privilege. It's never nice to be looked down upon, and the meaning "to behave arrogantly" slowly emerged along with democratic sentiments.

ROUND ROBIN

Like *kitty corner*, this saying probably resulted from the substitution of an animal name for a French term—in

this case, *robin* for *ruban*, "ribbon." (Why people didn't just use *ribbon* is kind of a mystery; it may have something to do with the fact that the English *o* is closer than the English *i* to the French *u*.)

Though *round robin* appears in print as early as 1546, modern usage almost certainly stems from the French *ruban rond*, "round ribbon." Officials wishing to present grievances to the crown in the 17th century devised a clever method of concealing the instigator of the complaint: instead of signing the actual petition, they would sign a banded ribbon and attach it to the document. Since no one could tell who signed first, no one could be singled out for punishment (at the time, beheading).

Taking their cue from the French but mistranslating the phrase, British sailors used a similar method. No ribbon was involved; they merely signed their petitions of grievances in a circle rather than in rows. The captain to whom the complaint was presented couldn't determine the instigator, and so it was sack the whole crew or sack nobody. Sounds like high-school gym class to me.

Today *round robin* means competing in a circular fashion (especially at tennis) rather than signing anything. Each contestant plays every other contestant at least once, as if in a circle, continuing round even if they lose. I'd like to explain how this meaning arose, but my head is starting to spin.

SNAKE OIL

Now just a figure of speech for "bogus remedy," snake oil was once an actual product, though it wasn't necessarily oil and didn't come from snakes.

The term goes back to late–19th-century American carnivals, where fork-tongued con artists set up booths or platforms to sell awestruck customers products allegedly containing snake oil, which they reputed to have wonderful healing properties. These medicines and elixers were offered as cures for every aliment from the common cold to a bad complexion. They were, in short, phony panaceas. As for what they were actually made of, only the salesman knew for sure.

Government regulation ultimately put snake-oil merchants out of business, but not stupidity. And so the term, first printed in the 1920s, survives as a warning to contemporary gulls who hope to banish wrinkles and baldness with the latest ointment.

TAKE THE BULL BY THE HORNS

The most likely explanation of this one is that, like *seeing red,* it comes from the bullring. After a bull has been shot full of darts and sufficiently worn down, either the brave banderillero or noble matador will jump on its back and grab its horns, forcing the bull's head down, which puts a real crimp in its style.

Some writers suggest that the saying originated in America and refers to the cowboy sport of "bulldogging," which involves throwing a bull by its horns. But Jonathan Swift employed the metaphor in 1711, well before there were cowboys to bulldog. Others trace the practice to Minoan Crete, which is almost too good to be true, as King Minos himself had a bully (the Minotaur) for a stepson. But the exact reference doesn't really matter, since bulls are

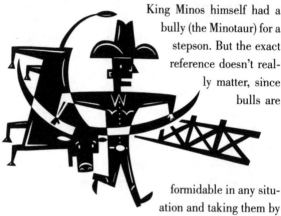

formidable in any situation and taking them by the horns always takes courage (as well as a measure of stupidity).

A TEDDY BEAR

American president Theodore Roosevelt may have looked like a big ol' cuddly stuffed bear, but that's not why the toy is named after him.

The heartwarming truth is that in November 1902, the president was on a hunting trip in Mississippi, an intimate getaway well attended by members of the press. A Roosevelt aide got the notion to produce a nice photo op by dragging a little bear into the camp for the prez to shoot while the cameras clicked. Knowing exactly how this would look in the papers, Roosevelt refused.

He made the papers anyway, in a political cartoon by the then famous Clifford Berryman of the *Washington Post*. Berryman depicted the president averting his eyes in horror from the little bear's rough treatment, except the bear looked like a stuffed toy. And the stuffed toy it resembled was a popular German model designed by a Fräulein Greta Steiff in the 1880s. Forever after in America, this toy would be called a "teddy bear."

The only complication to this story is that some sources, such as the *New Yorker* magazine, later claimed that the toy was modeled on the cartoon, rather than the cartoon on the toy, and that Fräulein Steiff sewed her first "teddy bear" in 1904. Another version has New York candy man Morris Michtom inventing the toy in 1902, right after Berryman published his cartoon. (Michtom made a real bundle, too.) It all makes you wonder whether anything in the story is true except that Berryman drew the cartoon.

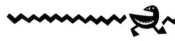

TILL THE COWS COME HOME

Now an all-purpose animalogy for "a mighty long time," this phrase originally (circa 1610) meant "until the early morning," which is when milk-laden cows, otherwise happy to stay away, show up at the gate for service. So "to party until the cows come home" is to carry on until the break of day.

Actually, most cows need milking twice a day—early in the morning and late in the afternoon, so the phrase might as well mean "until evening," too. In fact it has been used this way (as in "He slept until the cows came home"), but not as often. Either way, the behavior described is usually much more irregular than that of a cow; a more vagabond animal would probably have made for a better comparison.

A few of my sources also take note of what they claim is a recent amplification of the phrase: *till hell freezes over and the cows come skating home over the ice.* Personally, I think they may be pulling our udders.

TWO SHAKES OF A LAMB'S TAIL

Originally employed without reference to the tail of any animal, *two shakes* (or *a couple of shakes*) was gambler's lingo for a couple of quick jiggles of the dice cup. *In two shakes* meant "instantly"; *in a shake* was even faster; *in*

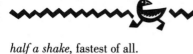

half a shake, fastest of all.

American farmers of the early 19th century picked up the term from common parlance and modified it in keeping with the kind of shaking they were familiar with—the wagging posteriors of barnyard beasts. Most rapid, by their observation, was the tail of a sheep set in motion; in the first use in print of an approximate phrase, S. A. Hammett wrote down the following in 1858: "Out come my mare, and in a couple of shakes of a sheep's tail we was a doin' our three minits jest as fine as silk." "The shake of a lamb's tail"—which is likely even faster—followed in 1867; Mark Twain went the other way in *Huckleberry Finn* (1884): "I says to myself spos'n he can't fix that leg just in three shakes of a sheep's tail, as the saying is? spos'n it takes him three or four days?" (chapter 41).

Two, however, is the most common number of shakes today, though *of a lamb's tail* is often omitted. Almost as common is *a brace of shakes,* at least in England, where one might still hear "brace" used as a synonym for "pair."

You Dirty Rat!

Animals are used more as insults than for any other purpose save maybe eating; it's certainly not often that calling someone an animal is meant as praise. The only truly positive epithets I can think of are *pussycat* and (in some cases) *dove*, if we except such compounds as *lionhearted*. I suppose you might call *fox, chick,* and *stud* "compliments"; even then the general direction is certainly revealing.

Animal lovers beware: what follows is a pretty grim catalog of the unkind and the downright nasty. But remember, it's human behavior that gives animals such a bad name.

By informal tally, I've concluded that the creature most often invoked as a slur is the lowly **rat,** as in *rat on, dirty rat, ratty, ratfink,* etc. And with good reason: rats are just disgusting in general; they're mean, they're dirty, they eat garbage, they hang out in bad neighborhoods, and they're very hospitable to diseases.

People have never actually *liked* rats, but hatred of them ballooned after the various plagues of the Middle Ages and Renaissance. (The rats carried the fleas that carried disease.) On the other hand, rats do prey on various pests, and their laboratory kin have partly atoned for their forefathers' sins.

(For the record: Though actor James Cagney is best remembered for the line "Mmm, you dirty rat!," he denied uttering the phrase in any film. "What I actually did say," he told the American Film Institute in 1974, "was 'Judy! Judy! Judy!'")

In terms of actual destruction—excepting the occasional plague—**weasels** are actually far worse than rats. These bloodthirsty little critters, who average under a pound, make a sport of death, ripping into whole chicken coops and rabbit's

nests, killing far more than they need for food. (They just like sucking a little blood from each fresh kill.) In fact, weasels will occasionally destroy their entire food supply, which certainly doesn't say much for their intelligence.

On the other hand, weasels aren't particularly sneaky or cowardly, traits implicit in our use of the noun *weasel* and the verb *to weasel out*. In fact, they're rather brazen and not averse to attacking much larger animals. What's more, weasels have a taste mostly for rats and mice and they're much more efficient than cats at keeping these pests in check. So you really can't be a rat and a weasel at once.

Skunks (a.k.a. polecats) fare better, if only slightly. To be called one usually means only that your company is unpleasant, rather than that you're dirty, untrustworthy, or vicious. Actually, skunks aren't a bad sort; they won't bother you much unless you bother them. But if you do, watch out—they'll turn around, stamp a few times, then shoot out a spray so potent that just a few drops can stink for a good half mile.

At the other extreme from these obnoxious mammals is the lowly **chicken**, famous for its alleged cowardice. Obviously, these are not the boldest of birds, but the reputation is a little unfair. Shakespeare seems to have started it; he was apparently the first English writer to use *chicken* in the sense of "coward," in his play *Cymbeline* (1610). By the 18th century the term was common slang.

"You assure me that Scrub is a coward," says one character in George Farquhar's play *The Beaux' Strategem* (1707); "A chicken, as the saying goes," replies another.

Such slander on the fowl, however, was not common until this century, when Americans revived *chicken* as a noun, an adjective, and a verb (*to chicken out*). Numerous derivative terms add insult to the injury:

- *chicken-hearted*—originally *chicken-heart* when coined in 1602; the form *chicken-hearted* was introduced by John Dryden in 1681. Synonyms include *chicken-spirited* and *chicken-livered*;

- *to play chicken*—in other words, to see who will "chicken out" of a risky situation first. The term dates in print to Ray Bradbury's *Farenheit 451* (1953);

- *to turn chicken*—first recorded in 1960;

- *chicken-shit*—American slang for "coward"; first published in Calder Willingham's *End as a Man* (1947): "You're both acting like chicken-shits. We win a batch of money—you're afraid to take it." A year later Norman Mailer picked up the coinage for his war novel *The Naked and the Dead*; and

- *Chicken Kiev speech*—a wicked pun coined by William Safire to describe a speech delivered by then-President George Bush in the Ukraine shortly before the U.S.S.R.'s disintegration. Bush proclaimed to the assembly that nobody should move too fast to dissolve the Soviet Union, which after all had been a source of stability.

Balancing out this dismal picture are *cocky* and *cock-*

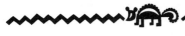

sure, which couldn't be further from the usual meanings of the genderless *chicken.* The former term—apparently referring to the rooster's strutting and preening amidst his hens—originally signified "lecherous," but took on the senses "conceited, arrogant" by the 18th century and never turned back. *Cocksure* is trickier, though, as its original meaning was simply "safe, secure" and carried no negative connotation. The *OED* speculates from the early evidence that the reference was not to a fowl but to "the security or certainty of the action of a cock or tap in preventing the escape of liquor."

More maligned even than the chicken is the now extinct **dodo,** a bird first discovered by westerners in 1507 on the island of Mauritius. Because it was a clumsy and slow-moving bird, the dodo had a hard time adapting to the march of civilization and thus became extinct by the 18th century. Not only was the bird awkward, it looked ridiculous, at least if we can judge by the models (none of them contemporary) in museums of natural history. Its appearance plus the ease with which it could be killed lent the dodo its reputation as a dodo (the word comes from the Portuguese for "stupid").

Off a deeper end we have the **cuckoo,** source of the terms *cuckoo, kook,* and *kooky.* But while the bird's call does sound demented (thus its reputation), it's actually rather clever. Rather than trouble itself to build a nest or incubate its own eggs, Mrs. Cuckoo surreptitiously drops in on a neighbor, lays her eggs, and lets the other bird handle the fuss (kind of like a surrogate mother, only without the contract). Cuckoo hatchlings like their stepsiblings so much they sometimes literally kick them out of the nest. (*Cuckoo* comes directly from the onomatopoetic French word *coucou*.)

Also low in the hierarchy of birds is the **gull,** long synonymous in English with *dupe*. The editors of *The American Heritage Dictionary* speculate, however, that the aquatic animal is an innocent victim of confused etymologies. Its own name, from the Middle English *gulle,* was at some point confounded with *golen,* also Middle English, meaning "to swallow." ("Gullible" people easily swallow others' deceptions.)

What a **turkey!** (referring to a flop or failure) is a pretty curious saying. It's tempting to derive it from the use of *turkey* to mean "dimwit," which is at least along the familiar lines of *chicken, dodo, gull,* etc. But in fact, *turkey* in the sense of "flop" goes back to the 1920s, while *turkey* in the sense of "stupid person" is about 25 years younger. And no one has a satisfactory explanation for it; probably something to do with how easily turkeys, like dodos and some Broadway productions, can be killed.

As for the word *turkey* itself, it was originally used in English (circa 1540) to name the bird otherwise known as the "guinea fowl," which an African native first brought to Europe through Turkey (the country). But when the

Spanish discovered a certain delicious fowl favored by the Aztecs and sent a few specimens back to the old country, it was confused with the guinea fowl (which it resembled) and gradually usurped the name.

Considering what we've done with *chicken, dodo,* and the rest, is it any wonder we have a word like **bird-brained**? The term, another of the myriad wartime coinages, first appeared in the British periodical *Gen: The Services' Fortnightly,* in January 1943: "There are as many birdbrains and dim-wits outside the boxing ring … as ever stepped around in it." I can't speak for boxers' brains, but though birds' are definitely tiny, they're no dumber than most animals.

On the more sinister side of feathered epithets is **quack,** originally *quack-salver* when coined in the later 16th century. The term is defined by these lines from the Jacobean tragedy *The Virgin Martyr* by Philip Massinger and Thomas Dekker (1622): "Quack salving, cheating montebanks! your skill / Is to make sound men sick, and sick men kill." The reference was to charlatans who loudly "quacked" (proclaimed) the benefits of their "salves" (medicines). These "quacks," as they came to be known in short, were the ancestors of American "snake-oil salesmen" (see page 123).

In the same league but even lower is the **leech,** a water-dwelling bloodsucker related to the earthworm. As is well known, leeches were widely used by physicians in

not-so-ancient times, when it was thought that many sicknesses were caused by "bad blood" and that the worms could "leech" a person back to health. In many cases this actually worked, as leeches could clear up a small blood clot or inflammation. And in fact, the name *leech* derives from the Old English word for "surgeon," which goes to show how honorable the worm once was, or how dishonorable the medical profession, take your pick.

Moving along through the invertebrates we arrive at **jellyfish,** which are indeed spineless, so the insult works so far as that goes. But they're hardly defenseless creatures; if you get on the wrong side of one of these floating disasters-waiting-to-happen, it could kill you. Each of a jellyfish's tentacles is loaded with poison and capable of causing a fair amount of damage. Even worse are relatives of the jellyfish, such as the Portuguese man-of-war and the sea wasp, the latter of which can kill some people in about half a minute.

More frightening to most, though, is the **shark,** which lent its name to deadly predators of the two-legged variety circa 1600. (Playwright Ben Jonson first used the metaphor.) Most familiar today are such expressions as *loan shark, card shark,* and *pool shark,* whose histories are thoroughly confused and whose source may be not the animal but the term *sharper,* a 17th-century coinage for "cheat, swindler, rogue." This was shortened to *sharp* within a hundred years, and one still hears the expres-

sion *card sharp* used as an alternative.

We'll pass over various slurs from the deep such as **piranha, whale, fishy,** and **shrimp** to return to dry land and to man's best friend. As noted elsewhere in the text, **dogs** are as often objects of contempt as of love; and no dog is as despised as a **yellow dog,** which has served as a metaphor for "coward" or "person of no account" since at least 1880. (The adjective *yellow* for "cowardly" is older, as it was used by P. T. Barnum in 1856.) Relatively recent are the uses of *dog* for "bad deal" and "ugly woman"; older are the insults **bitch** and **son of a bitch,** the former dating as an insult to the Renaissance and the latter coming into use by the 18th century.

Jackals gained a reputation as scavengers and hangers-on from their habit of trailing behind the big cats of Africa and Asia and feeding on their leftovers. But while jackals are the only canines who perpetuate the practice, all members of the dog family (which also includes wolves and foxes) once did the same. The trait survives in the family dog who begs for scraps from the dinnertable.

As for our other favorite domestic animals, **cats** fare slightly better. Their way of moving quietly and often tentatively, though, did inspire the term **pussyfoot,** which over the decades of this century has come to mean "tread too cautiously." In the same league are **scaredy-cat** and **fraidy-cat,** the former coined by Dorothy Parker in 1933 and the latter, probably older, being of unknown provenance.

Our perhaps too timorous feline friends cannot be blamed for **sourpuss,** however. While *puss* meaning in "kitty" is from Dutch and Low German imitations of the sound of a cat spitting and hissing, *puss* as in *sourpuss* is from the Gaelic *pus,* "lip," and by metonymy "face."

Since they're neither very friendly nor warm 'n' cuddly, **pigs** get an even rawer deal than dogs or cats. **Pig, piggy, swine, swinish, hog, sow,** and **porker** are just the simplest of insults derived from the family of *Suidae,* let alone derivatives such as **pigsty** and **pigheaded.**

While there isn't much defense for pigs' eating habits, consumers of Big Macs have little basis for acting superior. And as for the alleged filthiness of pigs and boars, it's a bit overplayed. The animals, besides being relatively intelligent, are actually rather clean, and only wallow in mud to cool off in the summer. As Ivan Sanderson indignantly notes in *Living Mammals,* "Just because a pigsty becomes a wallow does not mean that the pig desires it to be composed of excrement, rotting garbage, and decomposed bedding. In the wild, pigs do not excrete in their wallows."

Now that your opinion of pigs has been elevated, how about the poor **ass,** quintessential beast of burden? Relatives of the horse, asses were imported to Europe from Asia to do the work their more delicate cousins couldn't

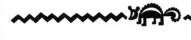

handle. Their name derives from the Latin *asinus,* also the source of the English **asinine,** which pretty well sums up popular opinion of the beast since the Renaissance. "Ignorant asses" appears in 1578, and Shakespeare helped cement the image in his play *A Midsummer Night's Dream* (circa 1595), in which the tinker Bottom is literally made into an ass.

Circa 1860, *ass* also became an American variant of the British *arse* (not itself an animalogy). Similarity in sound is explanation enough, but it doesn't hurt that the animal has a prominent rump. (Dylan Thomas coined the more precise *asshole* in a 1935 letter.)

Some word historians speculate that the animal's other name, **donkey** (intended to rhyme with *monkey*), was coined because *ass* had become too vulgar for polite speech. While it's true that delicacy would later demand *donkey,* when that term was coined in the later 18th century *ass* was still just insulting, not yet vulgar.

We've nowhere near exhausted even our short list of animal insults; we are, however and alas, out of room. The enterprising reader may wish to look into the rest on her own, though, so here's a sample:

baboon

badger

barfly

biddy

bookworm

buggy

buzzard

catty

clammy

cockroach

cold fish

coot

copycat

cur

dogged

eel

elephantine

fishy

fleabag

gadfly

old goat

guttersnipe

hawkish

hellcat

hound

hyena

coxcomb

crabby

cuckold

insect

jackass

litterbug

loony
louse
magpie
mousy
mulish
nag
dumb ox
roach
scalawag
sheepish
sloth
snake
sponge
squirrely
toad
toady
viper
vixen
vulture
and *worm*

Sources

Ammer, Christine. *It's Raining Cats and Dogs ... and Other Beastly Expressions.* New York: Dell, 1989.

Breland, Osmond P. *Animal Life and Lore.* Revised ed. New York: Harper & Row, 1972.

Evans, Ivor H. *Brewer's Dictionary of Phrase & Fable.* Centennary ed., revised. New York: Harper & Row, 1981.

Funk, Charles Earle. *A Hog on Ice & Other Curious Expressions.* New York: Harper & Row, 1948.

————. *Thereby Hangs a Tale.* New York: Harper & Row, 1950.

Hendrickson, Robert. *The Henry Holt Encyclopedia of Word and Phrase Origins.* New York: Henry Holt, 1987.

Mencken, H. L. *The American Language.* 4th ed. New York: Knopf, 1937.

Morris, William and Mary. *Morris Dictionary of Word and Phrase Origins.* 2nd ed. New York: Harper & Row, 1988.

The Oxford English Dictionary. 2nd ed. Oxford: Clarendon, 1989.

Partridge, Eric. *A Dictionary of Clichés.* 5th ed. London: Routledge & Kegan Paul, 1978.

————. *A Concise Dictionary of Slang and Unconventional English.* Ed. Paul Beale. New York: Macmillan, 1989.

Safire, William. *Safire's Political Dictionary.* New York: Ballantine, 1980.

Sanderson, Ivan T. *Living Mammals of the World.* Garden City, N.Y.: Hanover House, n.d.

Shenkman, Richard. *Legends, Lies, and Cherished Myths of American History.* New York: Harper & Row, 1988.

Stevenson, Burton. *The Home Book of Proverbs, Maxims and Familiar Phrases.* New York: Macmillan, 1948.

Walsh, William S. *Handy-Book of Literary Curiosities.* Philadelphia: Lippincott, 1893.

White, T. H., trans. *The Book of Beasts.* New York: Dover, 1984.

Index